Healing Times

Devotions for New Seasons

Dr. Lee Ann B. Marino, Ph.D., D.Min., D.D.

Healing Times

DEVOTIONS FOR NEW SEASONS

Dr. Lee Ann B. Marino, Ph.D., D.Min., D.D.

Published by:

Remnant Words

(An imprint of the Righteous Pen Publications Group)

www.righteouspenpublications.com

Book classification: Nonfiction > Religion > Christian Life > Devotional

ISBN: 1-940197-73-2
13-Digit: 978-1-940197-73-9

Printed in the United States of America.

JUST FOR TODAY

I WILL BE UNAFRAID.

ESPECIALLY,

I WILL NOT BE AFRAID

TO ENJOY WHAT IS BEAUTIFUL,

AND TO BELIEVE

THAT AS I GIVE TO THE WORLD,

SO THE WORLD WILL GIVE TO ME.

(KENNETH HOLMES, AL-ANON FAMILY GROUPS)[1]

Table of Contents

Word From the Author

He has made everything beautiful in its time.
He also has planted eternity in men's hearts *and* minds
[a divinely implanted sense of a purpose working through the ages
which nothing under the sun but God alone can satisfy], yet so
that men cannot find out what God has done
from the beginning to the end.
(Ecclesiastes 3:11)

I had no plans to create a "Spiritual Darkness Trilogy." I figured between *Waiting: Devotions for the Journey* and *Call Me Bitter: Devotions for the Hurting*, I had said all I was prepared to say on the matter. It wasn't until I was asked about it – and then the title came less than a weekend later – that I realized there needed to be a third installment, for a few reasons. The first, and most obvious, is it covers about a three-year period in my life. The second, which relates to the first, is that the number three represents manifestation in Sacred Geometry. This season of my life represents a period by which manifestation would not just result but would be intimately connected with my process. The third, and perhaps most relevant reason, is that this book proves God works in cycles, always working them through to completion within each of us. We can't skip the cycles, hurry the process, or "move things along" in our misguided sense of haste. Things take as long as they take, and our ultimate challenge is to slow ourselves down and flow with them instead of against them.

I think my biggest challenge with my seasonal changes is learning it is all right to find that infamous non-binary world of balance between light and darkness. For most of this season, I confronted a world of darkness I'd previously tried to avoid. I was quick to pretend it wasn't there or run from it in different forms. Here, God made me sit in it...much longer than I might have wanted (which seems to be a pattern for my various seasons), waiting out the time by which I would come to accept it. Now that I have accepted it, I work to find the middle ground by which all necessary aspects of myself are incorporated into one.

New seasons can be scary. They echo the haunts of seasons past and the simultaneous fears that things will be like they have always been as well as being different and unknown, all at the same time. We are expected to take the parts of us, both exposed and redeemed, and put them together in a new way. Our spiritual insights are different, and our purpose confirmed and transformed. God brings us to a new place only to show His methods of guidance remain the same: we are to follow Him, trusting faith will display the pillar of cloud to lead us by day and the pillar of fire to lead us in the dark of night. God provides for all seasons of our lives: those that are bright as well as those that are dark. As we shift from season to season, we are called to know that God is in the midst of them, giving us power to stand unafraid of what comes as we stand on the constant crux of change.

That crux is where I now stand. His guidance is my companion, along with the community that walks, stops, and encourages me when I can't see my way through or just don't want to go anywhere that day. I need the constant reminder that we sow what we reap and that if we sow to life, life – in all it often offers – will return to us.

I write this book in memory of Shawn L. Austill (1971-2019), Stonelane's Fiona "FiFi" Grace (2009-2019) and Gunner's General Gideon (2007-2022). I sit here, knowing the various seasons I spent as your wife and pet mama are over. Both those times – and you – and everything I learned in those nearly two decades will never cease to be part of me. I miss you, my family, even if I have assurance I shall see you again.

I must also acknowledge Nik, who is the one who called

out that a) my spiritual darkness series would become a trilogy, and b) is the one who called this book into existence, including the title. And of course there is Charlie, the three of us together who make Chaos Cubed, and in a year that brought the chaos, we brought the order. I love you guys. #hotarospiteforever

Also, where would I be without my awesome found family at Sanctuary? We've grown, we've shrunk, and now we grow again. Thanks for being part of not just this season, but many more to come.

As we wind up, I thank *Kingdom Now*'s loyal audience, now in the thousands several times over; my besties Julie and Lyle, and everyone else who cares about me enough to take the time to show such on a regular basis.

And last but not least, for Brad, who doesn't want to be mentioned and doesn't "like labels" but who embraced the most coveted of all: husband. Thanks for making the past few years great, despite their difficulties. Yeah, I love you, too.

Here's to the new seasons. Here is to change and all it offers us as we confront our anxieties and plunge into the newness God offers. Here's to God, who knows our end from our beginning: past, present, and future. Here is to us. Here is to me. Here is to you, too. Let's do this thing called life together.

One

ALL THINGS TOGETHER FOR MY GOOD

And He Who searches the hearts of men knows what is in the mind of the [Holy] Spirit [what His intent is], because the Spirit intercedes *and* pleads [before God] in behalf of the saints according to *and* in harmony with God's will. We are assured *and* know that [God being a partner in their labor] all things work together *and* are [fitting into a plan] for good to *and* for those who love God and are called according to [His] design *and* purpose.
(Romans 8:27-28)

One of my biggest struggles throughout the years has been private reconciliation within myself. Even before my late husband died, I experienced personal inner conflict between my earlier life choices and the subsequent results. I would struggle with regret: the little, nagging voice that in many ways leads us to believe things would have been better if we'd done something different. I'd kick myself for leaving home when I did, for getting married when I did, for marrying who I did, for picking ministry as a primary career (rather than a secondary one or something to do later in life), for pursuing ministry despite its sometimes abysmal results, and for the less-than-perfect responses I often had to the results of my choices. I looked around my life and felt that "better" was just beyond my reach, something that hid in dark corners of decisions gone by that could never exist in my reality.

Not long ago I visited with a friend I hadn't seen much in about twenty-five years. Seeing her again after such a long time made me think a lot about the decisions I made years ago and why I made them. Somehow, in some way, the experience helped me see why I made the decisions I made and how those decisions brought me to where I am today.

The choices I made weren't the end of the world. Did I like all the results? No, I didn't. Do I wish things were different than they were a lot of the time? Yes, I do. Still, as I sit here today, I realize something important: God worked all things together for my good. All things aren't good and won't always be good...but God, in the midst of everything, still worked all things together for my good. How do I see that in place? Because if I hadn't been where I was, I would be a different person. I'd have the same inner struggles and difficulties, but I would not have had the proper coping methods and support to sort everything out to completion.

"Better" is a misnomer we sell ourselves. It is a misty-eyed concept that exists in fantasy realms, one that focuses on what might have been rather than what was and what is. Choices are decisions we make considering the realities we face at the time we make them. We aren't given the convenience to pick and choose the side results of every incidental that may come along as the result of a bigger choice. We don't always have "better options" to make in our decisions. More often than not, our choices are non-binary in their results: they bring good and bad results. Those good and bad results bring a myriad of thoughts and feelings in their wake.

Some part of us looks back over our choices and believes if we did something different, we could have avoided the discomfort of our decision-making process. We forsake the good results and choose to review only the complications, not realizing that "better" is something that doesn't exist in hindsight. What does exist is the idea of different: our choices wouldn't necessarily have been better, but different. We wouldn't be free from consequences...we would just have different regrets. We'd have new problems to face, new difficulties created from our choices, and new reasons to feel like we should have done something else.

To say that God works all things together for our good

means we can stand right where we are and know that God is just as sovereign after we experience the results of a decision as He was before we made it. God is in our past, present, and future regardless of our choices. We see the results now, but He saw the results before we confronted our situation with our decisions. God has brought us to now, giving us what we need to stand, even if we have yet to get to where we want to be as we process this thing called life.

AND GOD SAID,

LET THERE BE LIGHTS IN THE FIRMAMENT OF THE HEAVEN
TO DIVIDE THE DAY FROM THE NIGHT; AND LET THEM BE
FOR SIGNS, AND FOR SEASONS, AND FOR DAYS, AND YEARS.

(GENESIS 1:14, KJV)

Two

ROOM TO RETURN

The sun also rises and the sun goes down, and hastens to the place where it rises. The wind goes to the south and circles about to the north; it circles and circles about continually, and on its circuit the wind returns again. All the rivers run into the sea, yet the sea is not full. To the place from which the rivers come, to there and from there they return again.
(Ecclesiastes 1:5-7)

Not too long ago I made a trip to Raleigh, North Carolina for a photo shoot and a "self-care" day with a friend. The Raleigh area was my home for ten years, all but the last six months of it spent as a married woman. The last six months of my stay in that area were both dramatic and uneventful, to say the least. In the wake of my husband's death, I didn't go out much. I spent much of my life trying to navigate the waters of widowhood: paying the bills, filing the taxes, handling the notifications, and making the trek back and forth to find a place to live in the Charlotte area. My last trip home was traumatic, to say the least: it was my final day in my apartment. I made the trip alone, decided to drive the "long way" to take in the final scenes of the area, and then clean out what remained of my life with my husband. Seeing the area's changes: cleared land, new housing developments, shopping centers in development, old businesses closed, and new businesses emerging felt unsettling. Cleaning out the apartment itself and feeling its emptiness as its contents were now in route to my new home only magnified the loss I now felt in my life. As I shut the door on the conclusion of that task, I decided I probably wouldn't visit "home" again, anytime soon.

In the years that followed, going back to visit Raleigh didn't seem like the best of ideas. I was afraid to do it alone. I expected the experience to be as traumatic as it was when I left. I talked about it on occasion. Once, about two years later, I was asked if I wanted to go on a date in the Raleigh area. I considered it, but the idea of having to return for that purpose in combination with where I would have to go seemed like a bad idea, so it never happened.

So when we decided to make the three-hour trip to Raleigh to visit the state arboretum for a photo shoot, I wasn't sure how I would respond to the experience. Part of me was hesitant, anticipating the experience to dredge up those painful memories and complicated years. I was nervous about it. I kept thinking about the saying, "You can't go home again."

The trip didn't trigger me at all. It was a great day full of new experiences. It didn't fill me with any melancholy. I found myself coming full circle: returning in concept, then returning back again, with room for a new outlook on the place I called home for a long time.

When we returned to Charlotte, we had a conversation about "home." Our thoughts of the day made us realize it's great to return to our "places of origin," however we might see those. Those returns bring up memories, inspire new thoughts, and help us to come to see and reframe experiences differently. It's great to remember, but "home" is where we are dwelling, right now. We can remember and visit, but our presence of mind is on where God has us in this moment, because the purpose in being where we are now is both different and the same from where He had us once upon a time.

The circular nature of spiritual life and revelation help us to see things have a way of coming full circle. The lessons we learned when we were somewhere else aren't that different from those we embrace now. Life changes and repeats, we grow, we change, and we walk the same walk, in different and similar paths, as we recognize there is always room to return. When we return, we find purpose in right now.

You can always "go home again." There's no prohibition on cycles of return or remembering, long as you recognize one simple thing: It's just going to be to a new home.

THEN I WILL GIVE YOU RAIN IN DUE SEASON,
AND THE LAND SHALL YIELD HER INCREASE,
AND THE TREES OF THE FIELD SHALL YIELD THEIR FRUIT.
(LEVITICUS 26:4, KJV)

Three

SO...PROGRESS

Do not neglect the gift which is in you, [that special inward endowment] which was directly imparted to you [by the Holy Spirit] by prophetic utterance when the elders laid their hands upon you [at your ordination]. Practice *and* cultivate *and* meditate upon these duties; throw yourself wholly into them [as your ministry], so that your progress may be evident to everybody. Look well to yourself [to your own personality] and to [your] teaching; persevere in these things [hold to them], for by so doing you will save both yourself and those who hear you.
(1 Timothy 4:14-16)

I was recently talking about a podcast in process with a friend of mine and casually mentioned the podcast guest was an ex-boyfriend. This led to a long conversation about past relationships, part of which went like this:

Him: "You dated some douches."

Me: "Yes. I did. I have faced my demons. lol"

Him: "And face new ones everyday offended by your message."

Me: "Lol this is true, but I don't date them now. So, progress."

When I said it, I immediately could see I had made progress. Maybe it wasn't the progress I hoped for, or the form of progress I wanted...but it was still progress.

The night before this discussion, I had a phone conversation with an alcoholic. Something about the conversation didn't feel right prior to the revelation that drinking six to nine beers in a day was considered entirely normal for this individual, but I didn't know what it was. As with all discussions with active addicts, the conversation takes a sharp turn when I make the simple statement that something about their habits sounds a little excessive. The goal of the conversation is to make it sound like I am the problem, rather than their excessive drug or alcohol use: suddenly I have made them out to be a terrible person (when I never said such), things are suddenly "not going to work out," and I "don't seem to like them." When I didn't respond to the arguments by remaining silent or agreeable (yes, if you think this won't work it won't), the phone suddenly disconnected.

I was all right with this, though. I have every right to decide I don't want to date or be friends with someone in active addiction. It's my right to decide I don't want to compete with endless habits, defend my position, or have an argument. No matter what someone might say, nothing was going to change my mind. I had nothing to prove. There was no reason to pursue something I didn't desire to prove anything about myself.

So yeah...progress.

When we think about progress, we consider it to be the results of the progress we've made rather than the realities of progress itself. We consider ourselves to have made "progress" when we are finally in that successful relationship, have that better job, bought that house, paid off the credit card, or done whatever the "goal" of progress will be in our minds. The truth of progress, however, is that we can't achieve the results of progress without first making progress. There are no end results without progress itself. This means progress is the work we are doing in each and every little step we take, no matter how minor it might seem.

Progress is a slow process, which is why we measure it by results. We don't have to wait for the results to feel its benefits, though. When we discipline ourselves to outgrow our old habits, our old relationships, and our old ways of thinking, we experience the results of progress. These keep us from trouble, from the pains of life they caused, and bring us to that much more hope that what we seek will be obtainable one day. No, maybe it's not receiving everything we want this second...but it is seeing the fruits of our effort, even if we only get to eat it one piece at a time.

COMMAND THE CHILDREN OF ISRAEL,
AND SAY UNTO THEM, MY OFFERING, AND MY BREAD
FOR MY SACRIFICES MADE BY FIRE, FOR A SWEET SAVOUR UNTO
ME, SHALL YE OBSERVE TO OFFER UNTO ME IN THEIR DUE
SEASON.
(NUMBERS 28:2, KJV)

Four

EVERYTHING OLD IS NEW AGAIN

I will [earnestly] recall the deeds of the Lord;
yes, I will [earnestly] remember the wonders [You performed for our fathers] of old. I will meditate also upon all Your works and consider all Your [mighty] deeds.
(Psalm 77:11-12)

At a recent service, Sanctuary sang *My World Needs You* (by Kirk Franklin) in the arrangement by Indiana Bible College. While singing it, I paid careful attention to the words and the honesty contained in them. The lyrics are upfront: the person singing acknowledges the state of things today are scary and they can't help being afraid of what's going on in the world. At the same time, they go a step further to acknowledge a powerful bridge of faith. What the world needs right now isn't another lobbying group, another online campaign to change politics, or another social service platform. It's not to say any of these things are inherently bad, but to acknowledge that without God, our efforts amount to nothing. Our world needs Jesus, and we can trust that when we call on His Name, things in the world do change.

I started to think about that concept of the power in prayer and the importance of calling on the Name of the Lord. When I got to the point where I said to myself, "We either believe in these things, or we don't," I realized what an old school notion such was. I had to stop when God immediately spoke to me, "Just because it's old school doesn't mean it's wrong."

I'm the first to admit there are many "old school" notions of faith that have hurt believers. Our attitudes as we fight current world situations have frequently digressed into battles full of perceived enemies and false ideals. However, this doesn't mean that everything we learned, did, or thought in those "old school ways" was wrong. Our old school understandings gave us powerful foundations in the faith to remind us how important God is in this world and that He does bring about change. Sometimes the change comes through a miracle, but often the change comes through us. God uses older things, older memories, older experiences, and older teachings to give us foundation. With that foundation, we are able to build, before anything else, better faith, followed by a better life.

It's great for us to take time, reexamine what we believe, and sort out the true from the false. It's also wrong for us to assume we are the only generation of believers who has ever had insight into the power of God. It's wrong to throw out everything old, past, or bad. From generations past, God has always called on His believers to remember their history, remember where they came from, and record what goes on in their day so they can relate these things to believers not yet born. Yes, this is so statues and ideas will pass from generation to generation, but I also believe there is something deeper in it. When we are willing to remember history, tell it, share it, and learn from it. With that step, we can also start to reconcile with our past.

It's tempting to throw out history, especially when that history contained hurt or pain. Through reconciliation with our histories, we can see it wasn't our entire history that hurt; only certain parts of it. This separation helps us see what we need to build on and what we need to change and embrace the power that comes from seeing God not as the agent of everything we always thought, but as our constant, consistent spiritual presence in the midst of what might have been traumatic or chaotic.

The more society tries to move forward without God, the more we will be brought to and reminded of older ideas and concepts so we can heal from our hurts and reconcile truth with today and timeless truth with tomorrow. Here, we find the timeless cycle by which we come full circle, only to find ourselves return with new information and power for the times to come.

THAT I WILL GIVE YOU THE RAIN OF YOUR LAND
IN HIS DUE SEASON, THE FIRST RAIN AND THE
LATTER RAIN, THAT THOU MAYEST GATHER IN THY CORN, AND THY
WINE, AND THINE OIL.
(DEUTERONOMY 11:14, KJV)

Five

MOURNING THE WORLD THAT WAS

And the mixed multitude among them [the rabble
who followed Israel from Egypt] began to lust greatly
[for familiar and dainty food], and the Israelites wept again and
said, Who will give us meat to eat? We remember the fish we ate
freely in Egypt *and* without cost, the cucumbers, melons, leeks,
onions, and garlic. But now our soul
(our strength) is dried up; there is nothing at all [in the way
of food] to be seen but this manna.
(Numbers 11:4-6)

The day after I officially moved to the Charlotte area I had to return to Cary and finish cleaning my old apartment. There were still a few odds and ends that needed to be transported and I had to clean the appliances, vacuum, and turn in the keys. On the drive back, I got off the interstate a few exits earlier than I had to due to traffic. The rerouted drive sent me through several back roads my late husband and I used to travel when we lived on that side of town. It had been ages since I'd been over there; no longer living over there meant it was out of the way. I hoped the drive would give me a sense of closure, of moving on. What I found instead was quite different.

The area I drove through had, at an earlier time, had a suburban, almost rural feel to it. Driving down roads and seeing new shopping centers, cleared land to build new houses and new business plazas, and noticing the things once familiar now gone offered me a whole new level of emotional hurt as I saw the world around me continue to change. It was so far removed from what I once knew, it made me realize that no matter how much I wanted life to stop, it would not oblige. I pulled off the side of the road, sat in my car, and cried. I didn't know what else to do in that moment as the powerful sense of loss, alienation, and discomfort washed over me.

After a recent situation that caused immeasurable hurt to many people I know – including myself – I thought of that day and that drive back through places no longer familiar. We often think we only mourn when we lose people, but the truth is that we mourn for many different things in our lives. Yes, we miss someone who is no longer in our lives, but we also miss the world that was our world, the world that connected us to ourselves in a different way when we still had that person in our lives. We miss who we used to be, how we used to feel, and the way things were as we saw and understood them in those times. We mourn the familiarity we felt as we realize the world we now confront is different, colored across different lines, facing different times and new challenges as we work to move forward.

We often look at the Israelites and their complaints in the wilderness with a certain level of disdain. After all, who sits around and laments living in slavery? How great of an experience could it have been if the best thing one can remember about it was garlic, onions, leeks, and melons? Deep down within, we all know the truth: every one of us has been in that same place at some point in our lives. The Israelites had new responsibilities in the wilderness as the lines of their lives were drawn differently. They weren't slaves, but on the other hand, they now lived with divine rules and expectations. Their new-found freedom came with a host of things they hadn't anticipated, thus causing them to mourn the world that was. If they were ever to be truly free from the lives they lived as slaves in Egypt, they had to see their experience from a more objective place. To do this, they had to grieve it in its fullness.

Instead of limiting grief to a singular thing in one's life, we must start to embrace the idea that we don't exclusively mourn people. We mourn situations, lives lived, times had, hopes and dreams that, at least in the here and now, will never be. Grief is complicated even when situations weren't and aren't ideal. As we mourn the world that was, we find ourselves more objective about them, which frees us to transform ourselves and embrace the newness of life that is ours in the here and now.

THE LORD SHALL OPEN TO YOU HIS GOOD TREASURY,
THE HEAVENS, TO GIVE THE RAIN OF YOUR LAND
IN ITS SEASON AND TO BLESS ALL THE WORK OF YOUR HANDS;
AND YOU SHALL LEND TO MANY NATIONS,
BUT YOU SHALL NOT BORROW.
(DEUTERONOMY 28:12)

Six

THE MYTH OF INDEPENDENCE

For as in one physical body we have many parts (organs, members) and all of these parts do not have the same function or use, So we, numerous as we are, are one body in Christ (the Messiah) and individually we are parts one of another [mutually dependent on one another].
(Romans 12:4-5)

Just yesterday I was driving my car down Independence Boulevard in Charlotte when the dreaded "low tire pressure" alert came on the dashboard. It's the third time this has happened in the past couple of months. Aside from the fact that the alert is annoying, it rings within me the sting of not knowing much about cars. I can stand outside my car and look at all four tires and see no visible sign of anything, even if people point out how low one might look. I have no skill to put air in the tires on my own. Every time something like this happens, I must take the car somewhere, ask someone to look at them, and rely on their expert opinion about what to do next. I must find people that I can trust to make sure I'm not overcharged or led into buying something I really don't need.

The experience of being single again triggers the temptation to gravitate toward toxic independence. The world can feel hostile and dishonest, forcing me to think I must handle everything myself because no one is trustworthy. Ultimately, that is the lie we are fed within society: the only people we can rely on is ourselves. If we don't know something or need help, we are led to believe we are failing as people. Instead of addressing society's bigger failing – that it's wrong to exploit or take advantage of people when they need help – we are fed the lie that if we are independent enough, competent enough, and able to stand on our own, we won't need anyone else.

The result? Whenever that alert comes on in my car, I feel inadequate. I sit and stare at it, with no conceivable idea what to do. It triggers a sense of feeling like I can't take care of myself, and such is a huge failing. As someone who already feels this inadequacy as I try to manage life with compulsive thoughts and a calling much bigger than I ever anticipated, I don't like the idea that I can't take care of myself all by myself. I received the message early on that self-sufficiency is essential; it is the ultimate mark of both adulthood and humanity. But the longer I live and the more I see life move around me, the more I realize the concept of total independence is a huge and taxing myth.

I recently edited and published a book for someone with the tagline, "Nobody succeeds without the help of others!" As I saw the alert in my car, I was confronted with the fact that whether we always like this fact, it's very true. God did not create us for total independence, but for community. While we grew up with the message that self-sufficiency is the way to go, truth is God has given us all different abilities. We need to have sources of support we can trust and rely on as necessary throughout life. It doesn't mean we are incompetent or can't take care of ourselves; it just means we can't do it alone. No matter what our struggle might be – be it mental health, emotional stability, physical disability, or something else – our struggles force us to reach out to others in our need and embrace the help that will draw us into community experience.

Independence is a nice idea. It seems simple and compartmentalized. It offers the promise that life can exist without the complications of human nature and the negotiations that come with relationships. We believe it (whatever "it" might be) can all be done all by ourselves. It also misleads us because we believe life is possible without others. We need one another's gifts, and we need one another's abilities. The true struggle of life isn't independence; it's figuring out how to live with one another, in community relationship, as we affirm one another's purpose without detracting from our own. When we discover this, we will find the blessing of community.

ELISHA SAID, AT THIS SEASON WHEN THE TIME
COMES ROUND, YOU SHALL EMBRACE A SON.
SHE SAID, NO, MY LORD, YOU MAN OF GOD,
DO NOT LIE TO YOUR HANDMAID.
BUT THE WOMAN CONCEIVED AND BORE A SON
AT THAT SEASON THE FOLLOWING YEAR,
AS ELISHA HAD SAID TO HER
(2 KINGS 4:16-17)

Seven

NO HEROES, NO VILLIANS...JUST PEOPLE

Do not judge *and* criticize *and* condemn others, so that you may not be judged *and* criticized *and* condemned yourselves. For just as you judge *and* criticize *and* condemn others, you will be judged *and* criticized *and* condemned, and in accordance with the measure you [use to] deal out to others, it will be dealt out again to you.
(Matthew 7:1-2)

One thing I've noticed as I watch anime is the complexity of its backstories. Unlike most shows that may only show backstories for main characters (and sometimes not even then), anime details the backstories for most characters in a show. This gives a complexity to the show that other genres do not share. By providing backstories, we see how each character got to where they are at that point in the series: who they are, what happened in their lives, what decisions they made, and why they are either "heroes" or "villains." Such offers viewers a unique experience. These characters become more than just players in a show, but real entities that reflect the complexities of life and the way that life – and time – comes for us all.

As I sit and watch the now classic *Fullmetal Alchemist: Brotherhood*, I have a distinct sense of the reality that life isn't quite as simple as we often make it out to be. The basic plot (as simply as I can explain it) revolves around two brothers (Ed and Al) who lost their mother, tried some magical practices they shouldn't, and now struggle to somehow restore their lives while dealing with grief, opposition, and adventures along the way. I think more than anything, the anime shows that no matter how noble or admirable a task may be, the world around us plays a heavy role in execution of any plot, plan, or idea. We don't accomplish things by ourselves. We don't accomplish them when we always hope we will. Goals involve steps and tasks, and as we go through them, we rely on the help of others when we get ourselves in bad situations or deal with opposition. It takes many to help us along the way, even if they sometimes don't seem obvious.

My initial response to several of the show's characters has been to dislike them. They might seem abrupt or brutal. Initially, we question why they act like they do. It's easy to sit and look at each character after only a few moments and make a split-second judgment about them. The longer I watch the show, however, I learn their backstories and better understand them as characters. They aren't as simple as the split-second judgments I might have made initially. The longer I watch and listen, the more I understand.

The reason we are constantly told not to judge others is displayed very well through different anime series: we don't have enough information to do so. We seldom know others well enough to recognize what brought them to where they are at and we don't know the battles they face, the adventures they are on, or the decisions that haunt them as they seek a better life. Sure, not everyone tries in the way we might hope, but we often don't know that well enough to judge. In every human story, we find a backstory; one that might not be readily seen in the course of everyday life.

Even though anime is animated, it brings with it a sting of reality that also explains its popularity. If we watch it right, it should remind us to step back before judging someone else. We should always engage in the brilliance of the backstory and let that remind us to listen to others more when they have something relevant to share. Instead of judging someone split-second, getting to know others either shows us their progress or needed work, and we can decide whether they need to come along with us on this journey, or we need to leave them where we find them and move forward.

When it comes down to it, there are no heroes, nor are there villains...there are just people, living life and making choices as they walk along their adventure and hopefully find what they need.

AND HE SHALL BE LIKE A TREE FIRMLY PLANTED
[AND TENDED] BY THE STREAMS OF WATER,
READY TO BRING FORTH FRUIT IN ITS SEASON;
ITS LEAF ALSO SHALL NOT FADE OR WITHER;
AND EVERYTHING HE DOES SHALL PROSPER
[AND COME TO MATURITY].
(PSALM 1:3)

Eight

HARD PEACE

Do not fret *or* have any anxiety about anything, but in every circumstance *and* in everything, by prayer and petition (definite requests), with thanksgiving, continue to make your wants known to God. And God's peace [shall be yours, that tranquil state of a soul assured of its salvation through Christ, and so fearing nothing from God and being content with its earthly lot of whatever sort that is, that peace] which transcends all understanding shall garrison *and* mount guard over your hearts and minds in Christ Jesus.
(Philippians 4:6-7)

The situation at hand had been in play for over a year by the time I knew I needed to call it quits. It wasn't what I'd call a happy ending. If anything, it was a huge letdown, one that left me feeling a strange sense of emptiness. The year went from an initial promise, to very good, to complicated, to questionable, at best. The roller coaster of uncertainty left me exhausted and searching for answers elsewhere, as I couldn't get them where I should have. All I had at the end was a strong sense of discernment that told me something was wrong. It would be that sense of discernment that led me to piece together what was happening just enough to know moving on was the right thing to do. I felt peace.

However...it wasn't peace like people talk about. It didn't leave me feeling happy and fulfilled. It was peace because I knew what I had to do, and I had to do it. The chaos, the uncertainty was no longer part of my life, but this didn't mean I was happy with the outcome. It was what it was what it was. Nothing was going to change it. I turned my head for too long because I hoped I'd look back on a different day and see a miracle occur rather than the hard miracle, the hard change God wanted to work within me. When I came to acceptance, I found my peace...an unwanted peace...a challenging peace...an unsettling peace...a difficult peace...a hard peace.

I think we often associate peace with the absence of challenge. We believe if we are in a peaceful place, we won't have any response to the realities we now face. It's assumed that everything will make us feel all right. We won't have to feel peace about situations that somehow leave us empty. Our hope, had in vain, is that every peace will be a fun peace; a peace that we will enjoy and will bring us personal satisfaction. We live thoroughly unprepared for a permeating peace in situations that hurt more than they help and burn more than they bless.

Yet in these places, we come to firsthand experience the peace that passes all understanding. The concept that God's peace can pass all understanding is that it doesn't make sense. It's not a human peace or a worldly peace, but an interior one that rests exactly where it needs to at just the right time. It doesn't rise in a situation where peace isn't required. If anything, it rises in situations where we shouldn't feel peaceful...and yet we do. It's God at work: omnipresent, omnipotent, and omniscient, speaking to us and offering us revelation of His presence in our most difficult times. Through the things we don't want to face and the realities we don't want to see, God offers us a sense of His hard peace as it brings us to the assurance needed to complete a situation, a cycle, or a behavior. The peace that passes all understanding is one of empowerment, of fire that burns away impurities and pushes us to do things we never thought possible...even if they are things that changes nobody's life but our own.

Ultimately, that is the goal of hard peace: it changes us. God gives us the assurance that He is with us when we are faced with things that force us to confront the truth about ourselves, others, and things unpleasant. Through the hurts of confrontation, we first deal with the way we would rather avoid truth and embrace beautiful lies. God comes to us through change, as change, revealing Himself in the form and shape of everything we avoid. There stands God, offering the hard peace, the peace that passes all understanding. We find assurance in the journey. We find hope when all we willingly want to see is darkness. We trust that even though we don't understand it, God is there, working things together for our good as we strive and trust...and hate every last minute of it.

I WILL BLESS THE LORD,
WHO HAS GIVEN ME COUNSEL;
YES, MY HEART INSTRUCTS ME
IN THE NIGHT SEASONS.
(PSALM 16:7)

Nine

I COULD USE SOMEBODY

Above all things have intense *and* unfailing love
for one another, for love covers a multitude of sins
[forgives and disregards the offenses of others].
Practice hospitality to one another (those of the household
of faith). [Be hospitable, be a lover of strangers, with brotherly
affection for the unknown guests, the foreigners, the poor,
and all others who come your way who are of Christ's body.]
And [in each instance] do it ungrudgingly (cordially and
graciously, without complaining but as representing Him).
(1 Peter 4:8-9)

It seems like the past year was, in some ways, more tumultuous than those previous since my husband died. There are a few reasons for this, the primary one being it is the first year I have made any attempt to live as a single person on my own. While the previous years were grief-filled encounters full of changes and adjustments, this has been the only year of them all that challenged me to experience life in any way, shape, or form. I cautiously edged into a serious relationship which wound up not working out, thus its end. I dealt with change in my ministry, including the departure of someone who was part of it for a long time. I discovered I had a form of obsessive-compulsive disorder. I met new people, made new friends, and developed a circle of support that was, in some ways, the first one I've ever had as an adult. I decided to take the leap and dye my hair black, transitioning from platinum blonde to very dark hair. I started modeling. I sold one house and moved to another. I lost my dog of almost fifteen years, rounding out the crushing feeling that the entire family I once had was now gone. It was a 12-month period that changed my life multiple times over, sometimes in ways that were quite exhausting and overwhelming.

As I write this, it's not surprising to say that I went through a lot of inner turmoil in those twelve months. Listing all those changes makes me wonder how I survived the year. It's also not surprising to say I came in one way and left another. Through many months, I lived lives that sometimes seemed like my own, but often didn't. It was safe to say I wasn't what I once was, even if that person was different across a few weeks in time.

Like most people going through a lot of change, I had the need to talk. As a person, I'm not the biggest talker when it comes to personal issues. I'd rather we skip over me and talk about someone else, anyone else in the room. It's hard for me to articulate my feelings and I must spend time thinking about a situation to figure out what they are. That process can take days to weeks, sometimes even months. So, to say I wanted to talk is a big deal. I wanted to talk, and I wanted certain people to listen. And, as life often had it, for one reason or another, the people I often wanted to listen weren't available. Whether it was due to work, busyness, or their own emotional instabilities, the people I designated as my necessary "listeners" often failed to live up to my expectations.

Initially, I found myself indignant because of this fact. I considered it the responsibility of very specific people to be there (perhaps, I was not wrong in this assertion). Instead, every time I needed to talk, there was always someone there to listen. They weren't the people I might have wanted, but they were the people I needed. Whether during the day or long into the night, the conversations drove me to self-realization as well as larger, existential thoughts that became important foundations for the spiritual direction I now take.

Everyone I clung to hardest – those I wanted to hear me out the most – are all, through the tumult that's been the past year, gone from my life. I held dearest to them while they let me go, not realizing the truth I needed to see until I finally let go, too. Sometimes we cling the hardest to the people who are the worst for us, hoping and believing it will all get better if we could just get them to notice our need. But if we are willing – just willing – to see who is really there, maybe we will regard ourselves enough to stop clinging to those we think we need and see we are already living without them. This is an important stage to our healing as we sit awake in the dark hours and talk to those who recognize how much we need somebody to listen.

A WORD FITLY SPOKEN AND IN DUE SEASON
IS LIKE APPLES OF GOLD IN SETTINGS OF SILVER.
(PROVERBS 25:11)

Ten

HI, MY NAME IS MISERY

Thus says the Lord to His anointed, to Cyrus,
whose right hand I have held to subdue nations before him, and I
will unarm *and* ungird the loins of kings to open doors before him,
so that gates will not be shut. I will go before you and level the
mountains [to make the crooked places straight]; I will break in
pieces the doors of bronze and cut asunder
the bars of iron. And I will give you the treasures of darkness and
hidden riches of secret places, that you may know that
it is I, the Lord, the God of Israel, Who calls you by your name.
(Isaiah 45:1-3)

When I sat to prepare my message "The Treasures of Darkness" for Sanctuary's third anniversary service, my focus centered on Cyrus, the king promised treasures in dark places by God Himself. It was a struggle to find out much about him, as most websites want to speak of Cyrus as a type of the Messiah, one anointed to rule and subdue nations to bring about the will of God in his day. As fascinating as all this theological insight might be, it wasn't the information I wanted. Then, after sorting through several internet sites, I came across a fact that stunned me: his name didn't mean "victorious one" or "happy one." It meant "miserable."

Cyrus the Great was leader of the first Persian Empire. History speaks many good things about him and his rule: he was an impressive military leader, he was benevolent to conquered nations (allowing them to maintain their culture, language, and worship), and he was influential in the rebuilding of the temple destroyed by King Nebuchadnezzar. There are twenty-three references to him in the Bible, found throughout the books of Isaiah, Ezra, 2 Chronicles, and

Daniel. He was appointed and anointed for a specific purpose, an example of God using a ruler who wasn't part of the Jewish people to execute His will. His legacy was, overall, a good one.

Despite all this renown...all this history...all this purpose...his name...is still misery.

Cyrus was appointed for a purpose, but that doesn't mean what he was called to do was easy. Tearing down, occupying, leading an empire, and being used as a source of force and might may sound like a fantasy win in a video game...but reality was very different. Cyrus saw his soldiers fall, the long-term effects of battle, and the complications of reconstructing nations while trying to preserve their own unique facets during occupation. It might have been awe-inspiring, but it was also heavy. Standing before all he conquered still raised deep questions about the meaning of life and the difficulties of answering a call that wasn't all "love, light, and positivity."

I'm from a church generation that assumes "positivity" is God and "negativity" is the devil. It's assumed if you don't feel upbeat, happy, and positive all the time there is something wrong with your faith. People assume if you deal with negative emotions or periods of darkness (depression, grief, pessimism, cynicism, etc.) God can't use you. We are so concerned that someone's dark state might call us to something deeper than our nonsensical platitudes, we degrade the people who find their calling in darkness as they try to sort out its heaviness.

Cyrus was promised "treasures in darkness" – treasures in his miserable state. Maybe they weren't the treasures everyone easily understood because they could only be received in his misery. As he conquered nations, I'm pretty sure a lot of people didn't see how his actions would benefit them. Maybe there were treasures, realities, insights only Cyrus received, ones that were so personal, others missed them. Maybe they were things received in those dark, long nights as he agonized over strategy and how to execute justice in situations that would forever seem unfair to others. His heavy calling merited misery. In a way we cannot easily understand, that's precisely where he found his blessing.

Cyrus and other troubled Biblical characters – such as Naomi, Job, and Jeremiah – remind us blessings don't always come wrapped in positivity. We have as much to learn and gain from those experiences of darkness – and the troubled people who experience them – as they embrace their valid treasures found in the hidden recesses of misery.

THE LORD GOD HAS GIVEN ME THE TONGUE OF A DISCIPLE AND
OF ONE WHO IS TAUGHT,
THAT I SHOULD KNOW HOW TO SPEAK A WORD IN SEASON
TO HIM WHO IS WEARY.
HE WAKENS ME MORNING BY MORNING,
HE WAKENS MY EAR TO HEAR AS A DISCIPLE
[AS ONE WHO IS TAUGHT].
(ISAIAH 50:4)

Eleven

BEING MESSY

But when the Messiah arrived, High Priest of the superior things of
this new covenant, He bypassed the old tent
and its trappings in this created world and went straight
into heaven's "tent"—the true Holy Place—once and for all.
He also bypassed the sacrifices consisting of goat and calf blood,
instead using His own blood as the price to set us free once and for
all. If that animal blood and the other rituals
of purification were effective in cleaning up certain matters
of our religion and behavior, think how much more the blood of
Christ cleans up our whole lives, inside and out.
Through the Spirit, Christ offered Himself as an unblemished
sacrifice, freeing us from all those dead-end efforts to make
ourselves respectable, so that we can live all out for God.
(Hebrews 9:11-15, MSG)

When I decided to make the transition from blonde to black hair, there were a number of changes I didn't consider. For one, I had no idea that changing the color of my hair would change the nature of the dye itself, as well as the texture of my hair. I had used the highest possible developer on my hair for years, and let's just say my hair was relieved to have a bit of a break, even if it was a huge adjustment for me. I had to use conditioner daily (as opposed to once or twice per week) and I had to change the shampoo I'd used for years. My hair was suddenly softer, I was more aware of its flyaway nature, and its texture was radically different. I stopped losing a multitude of hair strands every day and adjusted to a dark-headed reflection every time I looked in the mirror.

Styling was a different issue entirely. I was known to fuss with my hair extensively as a blonde. I was always combing it to avoid snarls and to put it in its proper place.

This over-styling didn't work on my dark hair. The more I combed it, the more I fussed with its layering, the straighter or more "off" looking my hair would turn out. I looked strange every day for about a month before I decided to try something different: I left it alone. I towel dried it a little and then left it to its own devices until it dried. There was to be no touching, no fussing, just shaking off a little bit of the water...and that was it for hours. Lo and behold, when I brushed it a few hours later, it looked perfect.

The hardest adjustment has definitely been learning to live with messy hair while it dries. I'm from the old school of thinking by which hair should always be perfect and not ever out of place. Towel drying it, leaving it wet and curling everywhere, with no ability to comb it all together has a way of driving me crazy. It makes me feel disordered, chaotic, even messy. I am learning to be all right with being messy. Then I realize the way my hair makes me feel isn't all my hair; it's the way I often feel about my life, and I am facing the same challenge as a person in this season of my life. I am learning to be all right with being messy.

Perhaps my biggest gripe with the modern church is the convenient way in which we try to avoid "being messy." We talk about it as a critical point from the pulpit and on social media when people are acting out of line in some way, going as far as to deem certain ministries and ministers as "a hot mess." But isn't dealing with – and learning to live with mess – a part of the church's call? We love the idea of huge crowds and sitting atop big ministries with millions of adoring fans, but what about the work that Jesus called us to do – that which is less than glamorous? What about dealing with the issues and problems people have, the things that need correction and calling out? What about those times when we must face things, head on, within ourselves? We tell people to come as they are, but when they arrive – issues in hand – we don't think to offer what they need because it won't paint the pretty, perfectly coiffed picture we hope to achieve.

We are so often afraid to get our spiritual hands dirty and deal with the hard aspects of ministerial life that we would rather skip them in the face of reality. Life is messy; so is ministry. The Bible is full of messy people, messy situations, and messy things so we can face our mess, work toward cleaning it up, and then start working on the next one...and the next...and the next. It's all right to be messy. It's all right to be honest about our messiness. It is not all right to brush it out of our face and pretend our mess isn't real, especially as it stares us all right in the face. I'm embracing my mess: inside, outside, and as is the case right now, on top of my head.

FOR THUS SAYS THE LORD TO THE MEN OF JUDAH
AND TO JERUSALEM:
BREAK UP YOUR GROUND LEFT UNCULTIVATED FOR A SEASON, SO
THAT YOU MAY NOT SOW AMONG THORNS.
(JEREMIAH 4:3)

Twelve

THE FULLNESS OF TIME

Wherein He hath abounded toward us in all wisdom
and prudence; Having made known unto us the mystery
of His will, according to His good pleasure which He hath
purposed in Himself: That in the dispensation of the fulness
of times He might gather together in one all things in Christ, both
which are in heaven, and which are on earth;
even in Him.
(Ephesians 1:8-10, KJV)

The ancients saw the world differently than we do today. This was especially prevalent in their concept of time. In Biblical times, people saw both life and eternity as cyclical, one flowing into the other without break or conflict. The cycles of life were divided into seasons, natural and spiritual. Natural seasons are approximately ninety-one days long, while spiritual seasons were understood to be indeterminate periods of time. They could be long or short, but in paralleling the natural understanding of seasons, it was understood that a seasonal experience meant something had been accomplished within that specified time frame for it to qualify as such. There were no seasons that lasted for a few days or weeks, but periods by which growth, life, and harvest came about slowly, over time.

Seasons can experience shifts within them. Things can go awry in seasons (just like nature doesn't always follow its precise form or order). Seasons sometimes run into each other, overlap, or resemble one another (just like sometimes springs are cold and autumns are warm). Some seasons are great, and others sting of lack or emptiness. While they follow certain spiritual regulations, they can also feel random and confusing. Relationships come and go, things change, life changes, and as much as seasons might seem like obvious experiences by which order comes in and ushers a certain feel, this may not be the case.

One thing I have learned about seasons: they don't make sense until they are over. When a seasonal cycle is concluded, one has reached the "fullness of time." When the Bible talks about this concept, it is talking about the completion of a cycle. All seasons at hand are completed to bring about the end of one cycle and the beginning of another one. All of a sudden, you can look back and see what it was all about. Clarity is reached. Purpose is understood.

We understand the fullness of time in the natural sense: graduating from school, getting a promotion at work, getting married, buying a house, or moving to a new city, for example. We can see what seasonal steps we took to achieve those goals and can understand the way those different changes change us, but we don't always consider the idea in the spiritual. This is because the natural realm gives us a material picture to pursue while the spiritual realm leaves us with intangible ideas. We measure progress not by what we physically attain, but by spiritual growth that isn't always obvious. We must wait for it, patiently laboring through each and every season when it's not clear what the goal might be.

In the natural realm, the world was prepared for the coming of the Messiah through the Jewish people. In the spiritual realm, the nation of Israel labored and struggled to understand its purpose and relationship with God. The rules didn't make sense, the periods of captivity were laborious and spiritually painful, and sometimes God's directives didn't sound the way they hoped they would. Yet when the spiritual cycle came to fruition, Christ came into the world. What didn't make sense before suddenly did, and the cycles were clear. The labor was worth the difficulty, was worth every season, and was worth every transition.

Now, we await the ultimate time when Jesus will return, and all things will truly be one in Him. It doesn't all make sense, just like much of our lives don't make sense to us. But when the fullness of time comes, we will finally understand. God works His eternal harvest in us, manifest in our hearts as we celebrate the fullness of times for us awaiting the final consummation of bigger things.

And I will make them and the places
round about my hill a blessing,
and I will cause the showers to come down
in their season;
there shall be showers of blessing
[of good insured by God's favor].
(Ezekiel 34:26)

Thirteen

'CAUSE...JESUS

And the times of this ignorance God winked at;
but now commandeth all men every where to repent:
Because He hath appointed a day, in the which He will judge the
world in righteousness by that man whom He hath ordained;
whereof He hath given assurance unto all men,
in that He hath raised Him from the dead.
(Acts 17:30-31, KJV)

If you've ever spent time in a conservative Christian church, you've probably heard someone make the statement that "Jesus is the answer to everything." Whether it's a marriage in crisis or a test at school or a bad day, it's common to hear that whatever is upset, bothering you, troubling you, or causing issue, Jesus can and will solve your problem.

Even though Evangelical culture tends to be a source of fodder when it comes to advice and general...everything, this is one area where they do get things right. Even though it might not be in the literal way they tend to make it sound, Jesus is the answer to everything. It started out as a joke, but now I have this habit of saying "cause...Jesus" whenever something comes up and I don't have an answer for why I am doing it that way or how it is going to work out. Why do I say this? Even though it wasn't intended to be a statement of faith, it is. In the end, I recognize and know that Jesus can and will bring everything to where it needs to be, even if I don't know how it will get there.

In the New Testament passage above, the Greek version of the word "ordained" is the word from which we derive "horizon." Bigger than the idea of something being set and fixed, we learn from the Greek that Jesus not only rules as far as the eye can see and beyond but is the focus of all that we can see. Nothing is beyond His reach nor rule, and for everything that happens, Christ is our full range, limit, and content of it all.

This doesn't mean that everything that happens in this life is "God's will," nor does it mean that "everything happens for a reason." We don't serve a sadist; we serve a God who is never beyond our reach, neither far away nor distant to our very need. Despite the things that come into our lives because of the fall of mankind, we are able to see God's sovereignty, God's reign present as we embrace the idea that Christ is, indeed, our true horizon. Our greatest focus, our greatest insight should always be the presence of Christ transcending everything we see as reality.

It is possible to get so consumed with everyday life that we begin to think life isn't any larger than what we see in front of us. We might not so consciously entertain the idea of idols in our lives, but where does our interest lie? Are we worried about our family members? Are we worried about our jobs? Are we preoccupied with our personal loneliness? Are we worried about money? Is our focus on our pain, our hurt, the wrongs that don't seem to minimize, no matter how much we try to shrink them to nothing? There are a million little ways that idolatry looks legitimate, even valid, as we minimize the grandeur of eternity into the people, things, and experiences we have that stand before us. Christ as the horizon of all reminds us eternity is bigger than what we think and feel right now.

It is our posture as Christians to see ourselves in the eternal picture. We are called to recognize the authority of Christ – Christ, our horizon – Christ, Lord of all – as more than just a nice musing to get through a test, a rocky relationship, or a bad day. If Christ is our Lord and our horizon, He is ultimately what we will see if we look got the bigger picture. Life's challenges should push us to recognize

Christ in everything, even when it's mundane or immediate. At the end of the day, we do everything, see everything, and overcome everything for no other reason...but 'cause Jesus.

THEREFORE WILL I RETURN AND TAKE BACK MY GRAIN
IN THE TIME FOR IT AND MY NEW WINE
IN THE SEASON FOR IT,
AND WILL PLUCK AWAY AND RECOVER MY WOOL
AND MY FLAX WHICH WERE TO COVER
HER [ISRAEL'S] NAKEDNESS.
(HOSEA 2:9)

Fourteen

CALL-OUTS THAT HEAL

To one is given in *and* through the [Holy] Spirit [the power to speak] a message of wisdom, and to another [the power to express] a word of knowledge *and* understanding according to the same [Holy] Spirit.
(1 Corinthians 12:8)

Not long ago I was talking with my spiritual covering/best friend about a situation in which I found myself. I told her how tired I was of dealing with it. I told her that I didn't know what I wanted to do about it. Then, almost without thinking, her next question to me was, when was I going to do it? She didn't shame me, criticize me, condemn me, or even make me feel guilty. She simply called out the reality that no matter how much I might have protested to the contrary, I was going to do the very thing I spent time complaining about. She acknowledged my weariness, empathized just enough, and then called me out to make the point that God still knew what I would do in the end.

Sometimes people use the word of knowledge (the spiritual gift by which God provides essential information either generally or about a situation) to show off or cause others a sense of shame or embarrassment over whatever they might face. That's not the true reason why God snitches on us, nor is it for this reason that we must confront the words given to us that tell all our secrets. The purpose of a spiritual call-out is to help us heal from whatever is attached to that word, resolve it, and move forward from it. Our call-outs don't always mean we have to immediately run or avoid that thing, but that whatever might be ailing us as connected to that specific thing – in any context – we need to be prepared to hear, accept, and start working toward resolution within ourselves.

Most of us fight God, even though we don't readily admit it. We fight what we know He is showing us for our lives, even if it is only for a season. We reject the aspects of serving God that require us to grow, to change in ways we don't expect. The work of God is fun and exciting when we think it will bring us to endless blessings, right up until those blessings come with conditions, consequences, even realities we dislike. It's easy to pretend that everything we do for God, with God, and in this life as pertains to God is everything we hoped it would be, as we silently scream and struggle for redemption from spiritual truth.

These places cause us to hurt. We struggle in them, endlessly trying to figure things out ourselves and fight the work of fate, when God works anonymously. We avoid the mirror of the soul that shows us what we need, what we are fighting, and why we fight it so hard. It's too hard, too difficult, too intense for us to accept. There, and only there, does God send us the word that calls us out. In that word of knowledge, we find freedom. In freedom, we find the will of God is as real as it was when we started to avoid it. It has not changed, but God, as change, comes to us revealing our need to transform as we accept His will.

The concept of our will as opposed to God is not as simple as we often make it out to be. It's not always about the struggle to recklessly sin or disregard God, but to accept the aspects of our faith that cause our faith to enlarge. Some part of us fears God's promise more than we fear our unbelief, for no other reason than our unbelief doesn't ask anything of us. In those call-outs, we are confronted with the places and parts of us that prefer our own comfortable safety to trusting God's will, no matter where it might take us. They present a sweet savor, a balm that lets us know God's omnipotence and omnipresence carries us through the things that are hard. Without shame or fear, we can trust that God lets someone else know our need so we can find Him within our personal hard places.

Then we realize when we stop the struggle and accept the word, the battle is finally won.

THUS SAYS THE LORD OF HOSTS:
THE FAST OF THE FOURTH MONTH
AND THE FAST OF THE FIFTH,
THE FAST OF THE SEVENTH
AND THE FAST OF THE TENTH,
SHALL BE TO THE HOUSE OF JUDAH TIMES OF JOY
AND GLADNESS AND CHEERFUL, APPOINTED SEASONS; THEREFORE
[IN ORDER THAT THIS MAY HAPPEN TO YOU,
AS THE CONDITION OF FULFILLING THE PROMISE]
LOVE TRUTH AND PEACE.
(ZECHARIAH 8:19)

Fifteen

THIS IS JUST A BRUISE

And I will put enmity between you and the woman,
and between your offspring and her Offspring; He will bruise *and*
tread your head underfoot, and you will lie in wait
and bruise His heel.
(Genesis 3:15)

There have been a number of times over the course of my twenty-five year ministry that I thought our ministry was done. Every few years, someone feels the need to not just leave the ministry, but revolt, as if leaving under peaceable circumstances isn't dramatic enough. When these times arose, I didn't expect we could recover or come back from the dissention, bitterness, or anger that resulted in decisions that had to be made. People tend to forget that leadership is hard, and one of the reasons it is hard is because people tend to personally blame leaders for corporate decisions. Churches and ministries alike are full of individual people who often expect their immediate wants and desires to be met, even if it's to the detriment of everyone else. When such situations arise, it's not uncommon for the individuals involved to do a lot of talking, a lot of very public and vocal protesting, and a lot of lying to anyone who will listen. Things that are inconsequential or often out of context or made up will suddenly become the drama du jour via social media.

The last time our ministry found itself in such a situation, the Lord took me to the passage above: Genesis 3:15. It wasn't the first time He's taken me to this verse, but this last time, something jumped out at me. In speaking to the serpent, God told him that her seed (Jesus) would crush the head of the enemy, but the enemy would bruise his

(Jesus') heel. Satan would cause a bruise, a wound to Jesus that would be just that – a bruise. It would wound Him and hurt for a period of time, but ultimately, it would heal. Jesus' blow to Satan – a crush to the head – would be fatal. Satan wouldn't make it...but Jesus would.

This same promise extends to us as believers. We may battle Satan's wiles for a period of time, but ultimately, he will only deliver a bruise. Bruises are uncomfortable, they are ugly, and sometimes they are sore, but bruises heal. Nothing Satan delivers to us can ever be permanent because Jesus already delivered a fatal blow to his head. Satan does not ever hold the victory because he is not the one destined to recover. He can cause superficial damage, but there is nothing more, in the long run, that he can do.

The very fact that our ministry has remained through these tumultuous ups and downs is a testimony to God's perseverance. Sometimes we get so focused on the immediacy of our situational discomfort that we forget it is temporary. There is no bruise we cannot survive. No matter how much Satan tries to convince us that the blows we receive are fatal, it's not reality. Survival is proof that God is with us through each and every bruise that somehow, we recover from, even if we don't see our way to understand how such is possible.

The concept of eternal life is often lost to those who believe we only experience eternal life after we die. If eternity is eternal, then we experience eternal life as much right now as we will when we find ourselves present with the Lord in heaven. Our survival from season to season, through disasters, trials, and things we think are the end of the world is a type of our experience with eternal life. We might hurt, we might not look real pretty, and we might not feel really great, but we make it. We survive, we heal, we keep going. We change what needs changing and we keep on pressing through the walk that is eternal life.

No blow will stand fatal enough to separate you from your spiritual destiny. This bruise, that bruise, and the bruises to come will all heal, as they always have. Stand back, wait for the moment, and watch Jesus crush the enemy's plans as you nurse your bruise with an ice pack.

A GOOD PERSON PRODUCES
GOOD DEEDS AND WORDS SEASON AFTER SEASON.
AN EVIL PERSON IS A BLIGHT ON THE ORCHARD.
(MATTHEW 12:35, MSG)

Sixteen

WHAT IF THIS IS AS GOOD AS IT GETS?

[And it is, indeed, a source of immense profit, for] godliness accompanied with contentment (that contentment which is a sense of inward sufficiency) is great *and* abundant gain.
(1 Timothy 6:6)

As *Good as it Gets* was a brilliant movie slated as a romantic comedy that's actually about found family and the role such plays in our overall well-being. The basic plot features Melvin, an obsessive-compulsive, bigoted pessimist (Jack Nicholson), Carol, a single mother with a son chronically ill with asthma who happens to be Melvin's favorite waitress at the restaurant he favorites every day (Helen Hunt), Simon, a gay artist who almost dies during a robbery (Greg Kinnear), and, of course, Simon's dog. These different characters all cross paths in New York City as life, or something like it, brings all of them together.

The movie plot is complicated, interwoven with mental illness, well-being, overcoming bigotry, and the way different people intersect in our lives and challenge us to be better, different, and more than we already are. Rather than a movie that depicts falling in love as a swept away notion, it accurately depicts the way that sometimes the people we need aren't always the people we'd pick of our own choosing and that love takes many forms, because it takes a village (so to speak) to make great relationships work. It shows that relationships often have many sides to them and that no matter how much we might inexplicably love someone else, life has a way of making us question why we are involved with the people we meet. As we go along on that journey, we run into situations that make us wonder who, what, and why we are here, and what God is trying to tell us along the way.

In the movie, Melvin's character asks, "What if this is as good as it gets?" Throughout my life, I have asked this same question multiple times. I'd look out over the situation I was in and wonder what I would do if things were forever like this. I remember the way the question inspired a sense of existential dread within me. What if life never changed? What if the people I knew, the challenges I faced, and the life I had were never different than what existed at that very moment? What if....what if...what if?

What if the question is answered in itself – What if this is exactly where we should be, right now?

Reality is that whether it's what we expect or not, change is forever inevitable. Whether it's changing our minds, our choices, or even our circumstances, change always finds us. That's why Scripture urges us to find contentment in all situations, even if they aren't always what we desire at the time. Truth be told, there will forever be something about our situations that we would like to change. God does this on purpose; it isn't His prerogative to make us comfortable. In discomfort, we grow. In change, we are challenged to become more than we are. If we find ourselves in contentment as we change, we see what God is doing in a bigger sense within our lives.

Many assume contentment indicates we don't ever want change to find us, but this is a misnomer. Contentment is acceptance, found because we trust God within our circumstances instead of seeing Him as a distant part of orchestration behind the scenes. Our omnipresent God is not far away, but with us as we learn how to navigate this part of our lives, embracing the people within it at this time, learning the many seasons of love that we find as community grows, changes, and expands, all within God's provision and timing.

What if this is as good as it gets? It might not always

be what I envisioned, but it's right now right now what I need: Community that has become family, love that changes everything, hope in dark places, embracing teamwork, and a support system that sits with me in the dark, no matter how long or dark it gets. If this is as good as it gets, then it's going to be all right. This is where I am, and that's all right with me.

AND SEEING IN THE DISTANCE A FIG TREE [COVERED]
WITH LEAVES, HE WENT TO SEE IF HE COULD FIND
ANY [FRUIT] ON IT [FOR IN THE FIG TREE THE FRUIT
APPEARS AT THE SAME TIME AS THE LEAVES].
BUT WHEN HE CAME UP TO IT,
HE FOUND NOTHING BUT LEAVES,
FOR THE FIG SEASON HAD NOT YET COME.
(MARK 11:13)

Seventeen

GOD PUT ME IN A "GET-ALONG" SHIRT

*[Let your] love be sincere (a real thing); hate what is evil [loathe all ungodliness, turn in horror from wickedness],
but hold fast to that which is good. Love one another with brotherly affection [as members of one family],
giving precedence and showing honor to one another.
Never lag in zeal and in earnest endeavor; be aglow
and burning with the Spirit, serving the Lord.
(Romans 12:9-11)*

There's a viral meme with two very red, tear-stained faced unhappy kids wearing one very large adult shirt together. On it is printed, "Our get-along shirt." The general idea of the shirt is simple: it's an oversized t-shirt that is worn by kids who fight with each other as a means of punishment. Until they can calm down and work out their issues, they must stay together in the shirt.

The reason a "get-along" shirt seems to work is because it forces communication between two people determined to have their way at any cost. Relationships of all sorts can easily descend into shouting matches, whether those disputes are literal or emotional. Let's all admit, we like to be right. It's easy to think those around us should be eager to cater to whatever it might be that we want at the time, and isolation is a thing. This is especially tempting if we are already given to introversion, and it can just be easier to do things ourselves...without anyone else.

It's hard for me to admit that in many ways, my ministry became an outlet for my introversion more than my need for community. Instead of growing outward, years of being unable to rely on others when I needed them drew me further inward and away from the necessary component of fellowship required for successful ministry life. I didn't trust anyone, I didn't have confidants, I couldn't reply on the people I worked with, and I spent most of my time in long thought-out decision-making processes. Everything I did, I decided – worked – and brought to fruition – on my own.

On the surface, I was an "army of one," as one particularly unhelpful member of my ministry once said. In reality, I was tired and embittered in the way I felt always left like I was hung out to dry. God's answer to this situation was simple. First, He removed everyone from my life who was causing me such distress. Second, He stuck me in my own version of a "get-along" shirt. All of a sudden, He placed people in my life who were there to help and made us all work together. This was a huge task for me, as I was not used to working with other people. I had to communicate. I couldn't be endlessly willful and do things the way I wanted to do them anymore. I had to learn to accept help and let other people do and complete tasks. Instead of undoing mistakes, I was put in situations where I had to work with others to avoid them in the first place. Things became bigger than me by myself doing what I could to maintain my work through the tumult of unhelpful and willful people.

God taught me about teamwork by forcing me to embody its principles. I didn't get a huge lecture or hours of preparation; nope. I was thrown into situations that required the work, the help, and the values and had to learn as I went along. God didn't gradually give me time to adjust my ideas and concepts...He Sparta-kicked me down the rabbit hole and into an entirely different life I never imagined existed beyond the comfortable walls of isolation.

The church is, in its barest concept, a huge "get-along shirt" for those of us who come to Christ in a transformative way. Human nature likes its own way...and some of us appreciate our way more than others. Instead of letting us sit at home with Jesus alone, God puts us in a body of people that are different from us in most ways. There we stand, in our shirt, forced to work out our differences and support each other when all we want to do is be right. Here we are, doing this Christian thing: one conflict, one situation, and each personal issue we have, forced out of us as we move closer to God and our essential need for community.

YOU KNOW HOW TO TELL A CHANGE IN THE WEATHER,
SO DON'T TELL ME YOU CAN'T TELL
A CHANGE IN THE SEASON,
THE GOD-SEASON WE'RE IN RIGHT NOW.
(LUKE 12:56, MSG)

Eighteen

ACCOUNTABILITY

Brethren, if any person is overtaken in misconduct *or* sin
of any sort, you who are spiritual [who are responsive
to and controlled by the Spirit] should set him right *and* restore
and reinstate him, without any sense of superiority *and* with
all gentleness, keeping an attentive eye on yourself, lest you should
be tempted also. Bear (endure, carry) one another's burdens *and*
troublesome moral faults, and in this way fulfill *and* observe
perfectly the law of Christ (the Messiah)
and complete what is lacking [in your obedience to it].
For if any person thinks himself to be somebody
[too important to condescend to shoulder another's load] when he
is nobody [of superiority except in his own estimation], he deceives
and deludes *and* cheats himself.
(Galatians 6:1-3)

I came up in ministry during a time when the word "accountability" was thrown around often. Ultimately, accountability was associated with obedience to leadership. We were expected "to be accountable" in all situations, but especially those that related to wrongdoing or perceived sin. If a leader said we committed some sin in our lives, "accountability" meant fessing up to that and taking whatever penalty was required. We were told the ideal situation involved having someone to keep us on the straight and narrow, sometimes called an "accountability buddy" who we would talk to on a regular basis about the issues and temptations we faced. In all matters, accountability was tied with confession in the face of accusation and punishment, regardless of what the circumstances present might have been.

Even though the communities I was in often shouted the loudest about accountability, all of us carried secret battles we knew we couldn't talk about. Our spaces weren't safe; they were riddled with judgment and criticism, not to mention we all knew the people who often spoke the most about accountability were often the least accountable themselves.

I do believe we should admit to wrongdoing when it arises, and that such is part of accountability. I don't feel we should be pushed or pressured into such, nor do I believe accountability should automatically be associated with punitive repercussions. God has also been showing me lately, in a way I believe is more relevant, that accountability is a greater principle extending to far more in our lives than just sin or doing something wrong. In a bigger sense – the sense God desires us to discover in our lives – accountability is about being responsible for our actions and receiving the necessary correction that heals when it comes along, regardless of form.

As the senior leader at Sanctuary, I am accountable for the things I teach. I need to back them up with sound theology I can point to in Scripture, and I need to be able to answer questions that arise. I need to be able to distinguish between my personal opinions and what God has to say through me and to me in Scripture. Before we ever get to the part about questionable teaching, I need to be responsible enough to do the job I am called to do.

As a person, I need to be honest about what I go through and accept the call-outs that heal and transform as I go through things. It's not about having a bunch of hidden sins waiting to jump out, but about the fact that I can do things better, and I need to be honest about it. It's not about shame or punishment, but accepting it takes community effort to become the people God desires us to be. Whether it's being reminded that self-care isn't an option but a necessity, that I don't have to hide the fact I like a guy or have a boyfriend, or even the moments where he will tell me I am doing God's work so that's enough of a reason to get up on a Sunday morning and get myself ready for church, accountability is a common thread in all these situations.

Accountability is created in situations where honesty isn't cause for shame. It starts long before something goes wrong, and things are done that we can't take back. It's found in each exchange and moment where we are safe enough to be honest about ourselves with others and know they will encourage us to be better in some way than maybe we were last year, or yesterday, or even a few hours or minutes ago. In that safety, we come to discover that God does care about the little things that keep us grounded so those big things don't call our names and tempt us to fall in front of the whole world. Community keeps us safe. Accountability keeps us real.

FOR AN ANGEL OF THE LORD WENT DOWN
AT APPOINTED SEASONS UNTO THE POOL
AND MOVED AND STIRRED UP THE WATER;
WHOEVER THEN FIRST,
AFTER THE STIRRING UP OF THE WATER,
STEPPED IN WAS CURED OF WHATEVER DISEASE
WITH WHICH HE WAS AFFLICTED.
(JOHN 5:4)

Nineteen

WHEN IT GETS REAL

Now faith is the assurance (the confirmation, the title deed) of the things [we] hope for, being the proof of things [we] do not see and the conviction of their reality [faith perceiving as real fact what is not revealed to the senses].
(Hebrews 11:1)

It was a reassuring fact to know I could miss Sunday service and Sanctuary would be in good hands. It was even more reassuring to discover more than half of our YouTube videos now had both captions and introductory slides. The moment when things got real, however, unsettled me. It wasn't because the work was undone or because anything went awry...but because I was identified as an "expert" on one of the summaries.

On the many nights I've laid awake in my bed, "expert" has never been a word that came to mind. I have always seen my life much as it is in the ordinary of everyday living. I don't think it's that exciting, nor do I think it's that noteworthy. I see myself writing words, putting together flyers, making slideshows, preparing sermons, doing Bible study, meticulously studying Scripture, history, and doctrine, counseling, and...doing a bunch of other things that don't seem interesting on the outset. I recall being asked what I do or what interests me and I'd often choke on my answer because as far as I was concerned, I was boring. Expert? Me? Nah. I'm just someone here on the sidelines waiting for their turn to come.

When I saw "expert" on the summary, it made me realize that I wasn't on the sidelines anymore. Sure, maybe from the outside looking in, things don't always look like much on a daily basis. I still do things other people do that may not seem exciting, but I am not doing them for the same reasons everyone else does them. I have spent a lot of years building to make sure there would come a time when I'd be competent and capable, worthy of being heard.

Yet while I prepared, some part of me didn't ever anticipate the time when that day would come. I spent so many years doing the "prep" thing that I forgot about the result. I was doing what I always did and forgot the reason why I was doing it in the first place.

In that split second, I realized things are getting real. Maybe beyond getting real, they have always been real, but I didn't see it. I was so busy living in one day at a time, in the right now, that I couldn't see any sort of future. But I wasn't doing these things for the hope or purpose to stay where I was forever. The goal was to get somewhere, not to stay put...but in my mind, that's exactly what I was doing.

Part of healing (at least for me) is recognizing more of who I am and who I have been all along, despite the different experiences that might sometimes speak to the contrary. Not everything is always the way it might seem in the eyes of our detractors. In a deeper sense, this is intimately related to faith and the way I live out my faith as I do ordinary things. The Bible teaches us that faith is both a substance and an essence; it is both the evidence and the ultimate thing that we aspire to prove. In other words, faith proves itself. Our dedication to faith is what makes things real when we can't see them, don't feel them, or don't understand what God is doing within us. If we will trust the process, we will find our faith proves itself, manifests our purpose, and brings us right to where we need to be, no matter what direction it takes.

It's getting real, it's real now, it will be more real, and it is forever real because it has been received by faith. There will never be a time when it is not real. I will just continue to come into a place where it manifests more because I have done the preparation. God has called me and by faith that I prepared for this time when I see the substance and evidence come together in the presence of every friend and enemy.

And He said unto them,
It is not for you to know the times or the seasons,
which the Father hath put in His own power
(Acts 1:7, KJV)

Quando n è un numero razionale $\frac{p}{h}$ (p, q essendo numeri primi relativi) la folioide è una curva algebrica dell'ordine $2q$, se i due numeri p, q sono entrambi dispari, mentre è dell'ordine $4q$ se uno di essi è pari.

§ 3. *Superficie sviluppabili in generale.*

Quando si sviluppa su di un piano la superficie costituita dalle tangenti di una curva Γ, questa si muta in una linea piana Λ; passando da Γ a Λ due elementi metrici si conservano inalterati, cioè l'arco elementare ds e l'angolo di contingenza $d\tau$ (epperò anche la flessione); di Λ si può pertanto stabilire l'equazione intrinseca e quindi dedurne, a meno di movimenti nel piano, l'ordinaria rappresentazione analitica. Il problema inverso, quello cioè di « determinare una curva Γ tale che, dopo lo svolgimento su un piano della corrispondente sviluppabile osculatrice, assuma una forma prestabilita » è indeterminato, perchè della curva cercata si conosce una sola equazione intrinseca; l'altra si può assumere ad arbitrio. Per ottenere tutte le soluzioni del problema si può procedere come segue.

Per la curva Λ si supponga aversi:

$$ds = f(\tau) d\tau . \tag{1}$$

Se i coseni di direzione α, β, γ della tangente della curva cercata Γ sono noti in funzione dell'arco s, la ricerca di Γ è ridotta alle quadrature, essendo:

$$x = \int \alpha ds \ , \ y = \int \beta ds \ , \ z = \int \gamma ds . \tag{2}$$

Ora, essendo identicamente

$$\alpha^2 + \beta^2 + \gamma^2 = 1 \tag{3}$$

si può porre

$$\alpha = \frac{\omega(u) + u}{1 + u\omega(u)} \ , \ \beta = i\frac{\omega(u) - u}{1 + u\omega(u)} \ , \ \gamma = \frac{1 - u\omega(u)}{1 + u\omega(u)} \tag{4}$$

ω essendo una funzione qualunque della variabile u.

Twenty

OCCUPYING THE UPPER SPACES

And the children of Joseph said, The hill-country is not enough for us: and all the Canaanites that dwell in the land of the valley have chariots of iron, both they who are in Beth-shean and its towns, and they who are in the valley of Jezreel. And Joshua spake unto the house of Joseph, even to Ephraim and to Manasseh, saying, Thou art a great people, and hast great power; thou shalt not have one lot only: but the hill-country shall be thine; for though it is a forest, thou shalt cut it down, and the goings out thereof shall be thine; for thou shalt drive out the Canaanites, though they have chariots of iron, and though they are strong.
(Joshua 17:16-18, ASV)

Joshua 17 is a discourse on the allotment of land among different clans (and one family) and the convenient way the Israelites wanted their territories on their own terms rather than on God's terms. God commanded the Israelites to drive out the Canaanites, which this passage reveals the Israelites did not do. Their disobedience resulted in constant battles with the Canaanites (and later, other surrounding neighbors, as well). God saw their end from their beginning; He knew that if they didn't fully conquer their land, it would never be their full inheritance. The Israelites, on the other hand, didn't see things quite this way. They tried to take the easy route and do what seemed most advantageous in the immediate, seeking their own personal gain. In the long run, they made things harder for themselves. They never fully took their land and their enemies lived among them and learned all about their ways, thus the enemy had a constant foothold for revolt.

Even in their rather pathetic state, God still gave

them a merciful out. As the valleys were filled with Canaanites prepared to fight for territory, God gave them the instruction to take the hill country instead. Despite their disobedience, He still told them how to have what He gave to them. When they weren't strong enough to take over the Canaanites in one place (the ones they allowed to stay there, by the way), God told them to move and advance in another area. When they looked too closely at the battle in one place, God told them to look and work somewhere else. If the valleys were too crowded, their focus needed to be on occupying the "upper spaces" that didn't seem too obvious because they weren't, at least at that moment, as desirable. Take what it seems like the Canaanites didn't want and infiltrate more strategically than attempting to waste resources on an area that isn't workable in the moment. Work smarter, not harder.

Before we judge the Israelites too harshly, let's step back for a minute and be honest with ourselves. There are many things that, when confronted with God's promise, we don't drive out of our lives. Whether these things are bad habits, people we refuse to let go of easily, or those pesky little thoughts, quirks, and ideas we have that tend to creep up on us, we also don't readily let go...of anything. We want our promise, and we want all the other things we hope will one day work to our advantage (God knows they won't, but we don't listen) if we keep them around long enough. God doesn't override our will and lets us attempt to manage the promise He has for us by taking things along that won't be enslaved, live peacefully, or go away because we've figured out this isn't a good idea anymore.

In God's grace, He doesn't abandon us to our own stupidity. With every battle we fight (every situation we must overcome) and most especially when things are out of control beyond what we can handle, God gives us the command to "occupy the upper spaces." Don't let everything go to hell but take your victories where you can get them. Take the places that aren't infiltrated, as accessible, or as desirable to all those things that we just had to carry along for the journey. Leave everything where it is and go gain ground in a different way, in a different place, somewhere else. If you can't conquer what's in front of you, move north and conquer something different.

God has already made room for our mistakes in creating a plan that doesn't so much avoid them as navigate us both through and around them. As far back as Bible times, God doesn't take away the consequences of our stupidity. He does something better: He lets us experience us in it and through it, proving that all things can work together for good if we will only follow Him.

NEVERTHELESS HE LEFT NOT HIMSELF WITHOUT WITNESS,
IN THAT HE DID GOOD,
AND GAVE US RAIN FROM HEAVEN,
AND FRUITFUL SEASONS;
FILLING OUR HEARTS WITH FOOD AND GLADNESS.
(ACTS 14:17, KJV)

Twenty-One

ACCEPTANCE

So Jesus said to those Jews who had believed in Him,
If you abide in My word [hold fast to My teachings and live
in accordance with them], you are truly My disciples.
And you will know the Truth, and the Truth will set you free.
(John 8:31-32)

Most of us know the short form of the Serenity Prayer. It is found on pillows, wall hangings, memes, and T-shirts. It is recited during every Twelve Step meeting, every day throughout the world. Many of us fall back on it in prayer ourselves, especially during hard times. Its powerful and simple words give us hope, focus, and discipline when we are uncertain what to do next. I think it's safe to say its short sentiments comfort us, especially when we need it most.

Most don't know the Serenity Prayer is longer than the few short verses commonly invoked by the world. The entire prayer, as authored by Reinhold Niebuhr, reads:

God, grant me the Serenity
to accept the things I cannot change...
Courage to change the things I can,
and Wisdom to know the difference.
Living one day at a time, enjoying one moment at a time,
accepting hardship as the pathway to peace.
Taking, as He did, this sinful world as it is,
not as I would have it.
Trusting that He will make all things right
if I surrender to His will.
That I may be reasonably happy in this life,
and supremely happy with Him forever in the next. Amen.[2]

It has become my practice to recite the full version of the Serenity Prayer when I say it. Every time without fail, I trip up when I get to one specific line: "Taking, as He did, this sinful world as it is, not as I would have it." I stop, I pause, and I think about it, maybe more than I should. Then I realize the very thing I am thinking about is acceptance and how vitally important it is to accept the truth in any and all situations within our lives.

One of the major reasons many of the religious elite took issue with Jesus was due to the fact that He spoke truth hard to handle. As our Mediator with the Father, He made it explicitly clear we cannot do this "faith thing" without Him. No matter how much we might espouse ideas to the contrary, there is no way we can fix all the things that are wrong with this world – with us – with the human side of the church – or of our lives – without Jesus. Acceptance of everything we see, we don't like, and we want to change begins when we accept the truth that sets us free because it helps us accept our limitations.

As human beings, we don't like the idea of acceptance. I believe this stems from the fall of humanity. Ever since our first human parents fell into sin, human nature has had an innate desire to fight sin in the hopes we can undo what has been done. The result is a struggle; our struggle, once again, to obtain the illusion of control and give ourselves the impression that we know better than God. We got this; we can change this dumpster fire of a job, or a situation, or a life, or a relationship, or a habit, or a thinking pattern, or poor self-care if we just push in and try to put it out on our own. In our lie of non-acceptance, things get more and more out of control, and we find ourselves at the end of something than maybe the beginning we'd hoped to find.

Most of the situations we face in this life require acceptance. It's a hard truth of "it is what it is," acknowledging both God's sovereignty and our humanness. We can't change the whole world by ourselves; often we can't change the immediacies we face as a result of sin, those things that lie in the choices and actions of others. When it comes down to it, the only thing we can consistently change is ourselves, flowing with the reality that God is change; ever constant and yet ever elusive in our lives. We hope we can change things as we want and when we want, but life doesn't work like that. We must wait with patience and move towards greater acceptance in the meantime as we wait for God to move in His infinite timing.

IT WAS TO DEMONSTRATE AND PROVE
AT THE PRESENT TIME (IN THE NOW SEASON)
THAT HE HIMSELF IS RIGHTEOUS AND THAT HE JUSTIFIES
AND ACCEPTS AS RIGHTEOUS HIM WHO HAS [TRUE] FAITH
IN JESUS.
(ROMANS 3:26)

Twenty-Two

STOP MY MIND, I WANT TO GET OFF

Humble yourselves therefore under the mighty hand of God, that He may exalt you in due time; casting all your anxiety upon Him, because He careth for you. Be sober, be watchful: your adversary the devil, as a roaring lion, walketh about, seeking whom he may devour: whom withstand stedfast
in your faith, knowing that the same sufferings are accomplished in your brethren who are in the world.
(1 Peter 5:6-9, ASV)

My mom has told me the stage of development we frequently refer to as the "terrible twos" is actually a period of disequilibrium in a child's life. Such is identified by difficult behavior that is a sign of growth and change in a child, one by which they are starting to perceive both the world and their place in it in a different way. During such a phase a child learns new skills, discovers new things about themselves, and is quickly growing and changing. In reaction to such, they are also unsettled, grouchy, anxious, stressed, insecure, and hard to handle. Both the child and the adults in a child's life must adjust to the changes, consider the reasons for the behavior, and help them break down both acceptable and unacceptable behavior as they experience both in their time of insecurity.

If one studies child development, they learn that stages of disequilibrium are as necessary to growth as stages of equilibrium. Both are necessary to promote development in an individual. Learning this makes me realize three very important things: Disequilibrium is part of life and does not end at a specific age; we need both ease and difficulty to grow; and growth is frequently cyclical, alternating between different periods of ease and complication.

For many years I found myself in a chronic state of "wanting." I wanted my ministry to grow and develop, I wanted community, I wanted friends, I wanted a relationship that was at least moderately serious, I wanted our church to be a spiritual refuge for people who needed it, I wanted to write a novel, and I wanted a podcast to have over ten thousand downloads. I wanted this, I wanted that. I made my requests known until I reached the point where I thought they'd never be answered. I went on with life.

Then I realized that everything I wanted was now here. Ministry is growing. We passed ten thousand downloads on the podcast. We are a stronger church than we have ever been. I have friends. I have community. I published a novel last year and am working on a second. I finally finished a religious encyclopedia that I've talked about doing since I was in my late teens. I am in a stable, very committed relationship. Here it all is.

And here I am. Now I deal with an entire circle of people who are always on me about the exact same things. Did I drink enough water today? Why am I not working on my fiction writing? Is it safe for me to drive in the dark? Why am I not sleeping? My own thoughts will then jump on the bandwagon as I worry about the number of tasks I must complete or the way my calendar is filling to overflow some days, while totally empty for others. I'm left with thoughts and ideas and a genuine sense of overwhelm as I try to adjust to the newness that is my life. Things I wanted are here, but they all snuck up at once, leaving with me a sense of disequilibrium.

As grateful as I am for the way things are going, some days I'm sure I'm out of sorts. Sometimes I feel anxious (although my OCD tends to give me a good outlet for it). There are days when I am tired all day and insecure. Some days, I need the reminder of who I am because my swirling mind hands me so many thoughts, I forget. The blessing of disequilibrium is that as I grow, so does the community around me. It's an adjustment, for sure, but the benefit outweighs those days when I am overwhelmed. Just like everyone and everything reminds me to take care of myself, so they also remind me who I am and that I got this, because in everything that comes up, both God – and them – also got me.

AND LET US NOT LOSE HEART AND GROW WEARY AND FAINT
IN ACTING NOBLY AND DOING RIGHT, FOR IN DUE TIME
AND AT THE APPOINTED SEASON WE SHALL REAP,
IF WE DO NOT LOOSEN AND RELAX OUR COURAGE AND FAINT.
(GALATIANS 6:9)

Twenty-Three

STAND STILL AND LET GOD MOVE

Whether it be for correction or for His earth [generally] or for His mercy *and* loving-kindness, He causes it to come. Hear this, O Job; stand still and consider the wondrous works of God. (Job 37:14)

The first worship dance routine I ever did was to *Stand Still* by the Isaacs. Even though I'm not much for country-sounding music, the lyrics of this song spoke to me enough to create steps and motions to go with its words. I would go on to perform this singular dance three different times in two states over the next few years, with the routine reworked and expanded over time. Even though it's been a number of years since I've done worship dance in church, I still remember each step to that routine. Through that dance, I gave physical form to my own struggles with God as He told me to stand still and let Him move. All I wanted to do was move things along, hurry them up, and be in a different place than I was.

I'd love to say I am further along on knowing when to stand still and let God move than I was when I first developed my dance routine eleven years ago, but I admit, sometimes I'm not. Sometimes my mind does the same flip-flop routines to try and speed things up, I throw the same old tantrums in prayer, and I find myself attempting to bargain with God in the vain hopes that whatever I want today will manifest tomorrow (or sooner, if such is possible).

God doesn't give me what I want because He wants to teach me something more relevant. When God teaches us to be still, He is teaching us to embrace eternity right where we are. In those moments when we start to measure time by our immediate understanding, God forces us to stand still and feel time in an eternal perspective rather than a timeline.

The English equivalent of God's Name – I AM – fails to represent the eternity present within its meaning in Hebrew. A more literal rendering of the Name "I AM" is actually "I was what I was, I am what I am, I will be that which I will be." In a singular statement, God is reminding His people that He is eternal, outside of time and outside of existence. He is not beholden to the standards of time we have established; thus, He doesn't move according to them. The God of all creation, of all eternity, who holds all time within Himself, loves and cares enough about us to sometimes stop our hustle, stop our timelines, and stop our haste and make us pause to peek at just a little bit of eternity in the midst of our short-sighted experiences.

There, as we wait, we stand. We feel our limitations, our humanness, our inner anxieties coming to the surface. In sight of the eternal picture, we feel small, almost nonexistent. When we experience eternity, God makes us confront ourselves. We learn He is God, and we are not in a personal, understandable way that leads us to lean on and rely on Him more. Through such an experience we can trust His provision as well as His timing because we come to feel the end from the beginning for ourselves.

The struggle moves through us as we vie for a control that is not ours to have. Then we reach the point of ultimate surrender where we stand and feel God move. Maybe we don't feel God move in a literal sense, but I would describe it much as we talk about the wind; almost as the blowing force that moves around us, but we can't see it beyond its effects. We know God is there and He is not just there for us but is also for us.

Waiting out God's timing on things is never easy, but it is the way He draws us into deeper relationship with Him. If we never wait, we never experience that taste of eternity that awaits us when we find ourselves together with Him on the other side of heaven. In waiting, we stop. In leaning on God, we discover the power of I AM right now, no longer looking to yesterday or tomorrow...but living only in right now.

PRAY AT ALL TIMES (ON EVERY OCCASION, IN EVERY SEASON) IN THE SPIRIT, WITH ALL [MANNER OF] PRAYER AND ENTREATY. TO THAT END KEEP ALERT AND WATCH WITH STRONG PURPOSE AND PERSEVERANCE, INTERCEDING IN BEHALF OF ALL THE SAINTS (GOD'S CONSECRATED PEOPLE).

(EPHESIANS 6:18)

Twenty-Four

TRANSFORMING THE BITTER PART

For everyone shall be salted with fire.
Salt is good (beneficial), but if salt has lost its saltness, how will you restore [the saltness to] it? Have salt within yourselves, and be at peace *and* live in harmony with one another.
(Mark 9:49-50)

My book, *Call Me Bitter: Devotions for the Hurting* was written in a bold and honest place I never planned to go in my writing. I had no intention of writing a follow-up companion to my book *Waiting: Devotions for the Journey* until I realized I was still experiencing several different emotions to what seemed like a life in flux all the time. In it, I explore the world of bitter places, those where we process trauma, hurt, and feelings often deemed as "negative" (such as anger, sadness, discomfort, emptiness, frustration, helplessness, fear, guilt, and loneliness). In so doing, I came to find God in my situation in a deeper way than I ever had before in my life. Instead of fighting and waiting to feel the way I used to, I came to a place of accepting my life was now different. Even though it was different, God was in no way distant or absent from me. Through my state deemed "negative," I found a discussion both with and about God I could never have found if I was in a better place.

When I wrote *Call Me Bitter*, I never expected I would find myself in a place that was anything but bitter ever again. This might sound dramatic, but my overly existential mind was so immersed in the world of the bitterness I felt (and all that went along with it) I forgot what it was like to be much of anything else. They say people with disorders such as OCD and major depression often feel loss more intensely, not to mention it takes longer to process than it might someone else. I am no different. I haven't just felt bitterness as a random combination of emotions; I've lived with it. It was my closest companion, one that didn't leave room to feel or experience much else in life.

Much like I observed Naomi's life had a way of resolving her bitter place all on its own, I came to find the same thing within myself. She wasn't so much changed as she was transformed into something that was not so bitter, something that saw light and hope and life again after great loss. It didn't come about because people told her to cheer up or tried to make her feel different about her situation, but because over time, life had a way of moving her into a different cycle. When she saw life change, she began to feel and experience things that would take her to a place she previously thought impossible in the face of her bitter, unhappy experience.

Salt is used to illustrate several different things in the Bible: loyalty, permanence, durability, fidelity, usefulness, value, and purification. It is representative of our faith in its many different stages and cycles; times when it's easy, times when it is difficult, and above all, when it needs and requires transformation. Salt reminds us of our connection to God when we hurt, when we need hope, and most of all, when we need change.

In Naomi's experience, I see metaphorical "salt." Her hurt didn't cause her to abandon her faith, but it did transform it. We can see her faith in her loyalty, her permanence to divine plan, being durable, faithful, useful, valuable, and ultimately, being purified. One thing I learned from watching cooking shoes is that salt removes bitterness. Through our life cycles (both natural and spiritual), God takes our bitter places and transforms them. As we walk in the imagery of salt, it is that spiritual salt that transforms us. It is through this cycle that we find ourselves able to stand as the salt of the earth: flavorful, rich, and good for the purpose of proving that in the most difficult of circumstances, life goes on; even when we don't want it to. Even when we can't imagine it would. If we let our faith work within us, our bitterness finds life once again.

BUT AS TO THE SUITABLE TIMES AND THE PRECISE SEASONS AND
DATES, BRETHREN, YOU HAVE NO NECESSITY
FOR ANYTHING BEING WRITTEN TO YOU.
(1 THESSALONIANS 5:1)

Twenty-Five

FULL CIRCLE

Though I walk in the midst of trouble, You will revive me;
You will stretch forth Your hand against the wrath
of my enemies, and Your right hand will save me.
The Lord will perfect that which concerns me; Your mercy and
loving-kindness, O Lord, endure forever—forsake not
the works of Your own hands.
(Psalm 138:7-8)

My "full circle" lesson was originally about dating again after breaking up with my ex-boyfriend. When I discovered he was behaving less-than-honorably with his ex-girlfriend, it was time to move on. In doing so, one of the first things I did – when I was ready to do it – was download the dating app where he and I met in August of 2021. I was going to talk about coming around full circle, completing a cycle, and so on and so forth. The problem with this idea is that while that might have indicated I completed a cycle, I was right back where I started from...and that's exactly how I felt. I didn't feel complete. I felt like I never left the beginning.

Fast-forward to today, I realize this devotion needs to be about a different situation. It, much like the other one, was a situation where (at least in the early stages of it) I felt like I was no further along than I once was. Sanctuary had struggled and battled with one of our members for over a year in different ways as the situation gained intensity and caused further hurt. No matter what I did, the situation wasn't going to have what I called a "happy ending." There was no option but to separate: her to the life she desired, and the rest of us, to begin the long process to heal as we lost our friend, a spiritual colleague, and I lost a spiritual daughter.

The situation worsened as she lied on social media about what happened, exaggerating and inventing fabrications that never occurred. Texts, emails, and Facebook posts made everyone involved sound like they were at fault but not her, with much of the blame placed on me. I was painted to be a horrible, controlling leader when that wasn't the case, nor was it what happened, at all. We were all left to live with the reality that for, at least this time, we were the only ones who knew what happened – and to sit in that while we waited for the truth to come out.

Through this long process, all of us involved have gone through a vast number of emotions and responses. Today we learned of her latest antics that now include different details than she originally claimed and her own testimony of her need to heal. There was something different in our responses, though, than in previous times. Every response was in union that her claims remain unfounded, but we were also able to see things we've said would happen in plain view in between her obvious need for new attention. I also noticed a general change in our responses. We knew where she was lying, but we also saw God at work. She needed to move on so we could all heal from the complicated situation that wasn't going to get better. If she found what she needed in her new circumstances, we were all right with that.

We've all reached a place of resolution. What is to come, no one knows, but we are content with where we are at right now. Despite our painful process, God is still moving within each and every one of our lives. God is moving in our church, and we are better than we have ever been. Things might not have turned out like we wanted in that situation, but we can see they turned out the way they had to. We trusted God, and He has brought us through.

Resolution bespeaks coming full circle with it. We aren't quite where we started out, but we are definitely in a new place with our new beginnings. Instead of running from our feelings or criticizing us for them, God has been with us through them. With every tear, every tantrum, every thought, and every conversation, God never left us. The cycle has completed, and we can now move on to everything He foresaw when this situation first began. We are good because God is good; He was good enough to wrap us in His arms, to hold one another as we cried, and to support us in His grace in a way only He can.

AD NOW YE KNOW THAT WHICH RESTRAINETH,
TO THE END THAT HE MAY BE REVEALED IN HIS OWN SEASON.
(2 THESSALONIANS 2:6)

Twenty-Six

HEALING AND HURTING

Have mercy on me *and* be gracious to me, O Lord,
for I am weak (faint and withered away); O Lord, heal me,
for my bones are troubled. My [inner] self [as well as my body] is
also exceedingly disturbed *and* troubled. But You, O Lord, how
long [until You return and speak peace to me]?
Return [to my relief], O Lord, deliver my life; save me
for the sake of Your steadfast love *and* mercy.
(Psalm 6:2-4)

We first started thinking about healing from life's issues in the 1990s. It turned into a major push for betterment into a compulsion for an abstract concept of "healing." In hindsight, it became a toxic push to be rid of things without considering a couple of facts: first, being rid of that thing might not be possible, and second, healing processes are difficult. In and of itself, healing from things can be disorienting.

We were given the message that healing meant we had to be over, beyond, and gone from everything that was hard for us to deal with or accept. If we had any trace of difficulty, we were criticized for not being as healed as we thought we were and pushed to do more examinations for healing. This never-ending cycle had a way of making me (and countless others) feel as if we were failures in our healing process. The hurt we felt didn't magically go away because we saw our situations differently. The hurt continued to hurt and when confronted with that reality, no amount of talking, introspection, therapeutic work, or insight seemed to make it any different than what it was.

It's a myth that we must be either healed or hurt. We

can be both at once: healing and hurting. I am also learning these days that sometimes it is our hurt that heals us. That painful process – confronting those things we would rather ignore or deny – is sometimes where our healing lies. We see things for what they are instead of how we feel about them, and we can come to a place where the very things that hurt are the things that go on to set us free.

I will say this is not true of every circumstance that presents itself when we are healing. I will also say that sometimes the most difficult things to confront are the very things that heal us the most. Rather than seeing healing as a punitive process, we need to embrace it as one of honesty, a place where we learn about ourselves, our experiences, and the different ways we perceive such things. In our hurt, we recognize the truth. In truth, we find freedom.

In Biblical times, the School of the Prophets was somewhere between thirty and thirty-three years long. In this fact, it's obvious the ancients knew something about the processes of life that we hope to ignore in modern society. As we go along in our lives, things change the way we perceive our spirituality. The ancients knew traumatic times, emotional disturbances, and difficult emotions would be part of life. That's why they established a continual school of support and accountability for the people who spoke God's Word to the people and leaders of Israel. They needed the time and the focus not to pretend things didn't happen or that things would be once and done in people's lives, but to learn how to live with the difficulties that came about from both the hurt that heals and the difficult place where healing and hurt are simultaneous realities. They hurt and they led, and they hurt while they led as much as leading while they were hurt. Never once were they penalized or condemned...but living life as they adjusted to their new normal.

I'm still working on it all. It's not once and done thing.

The longer I live, I see the consistent adjustment that life often requires. It's uncomfortable and inconvenient and disorienting and healing, all at once. Our freedom isn't in acting as if things don't bother us or living as if they never did but walking in the truth that they happened and they have changed us, which is what healing is supposed to provide. I am not what I once was, and that's all right. My hurt is healing me as I heal, and hurt, and move forward, and sometimes go backwards, and live, all at once.

PREACH THE WORD;
BE URGENT IN SEASON, OUT OF SEASON;
REPROVE, REBUKE, EXHORT,
WITH ALL LONGSUFFERING AND TEACHING.
(2 TIMOTHY 4:2, ASV)

Twenty-Seven

PHOENIX RISING

Even when we were dead (slain) by [our own] shortcomings *and* trespasses, He made us alive together in fellowship *and* in union with Christ; [He gave us the very life of Christ Himself, the same new life with which He quickened Him, for] it is by grace (His favor and mercy which you did not deserve) that you are saved (delivered from judgment and made partakers of Christ's salvation). And He raised us up together with Him and made us sit down together [giving us joint seating with Him] in the heavenly sphere [by virtue of our being] in Christ Jesus (the Messiah, the Anointed One). He did this that He might clearly demonstrate through the ages to come the immeasurable (limitless, surpassing) riches of His free grace (His unmerited favor) in [His] kindness *and* goodness of heart toward us in Christ Jesus.
(Ephesians 2:5-7)

There's a meme I see periodically on social media that speaks loudly to me. It says:

Some nights, the wolf inside of me shrinks to nothing, she bares her teeth and runs away. The dragon in my chest rejects me, she's so tired of being slain. There are nights when the lioness cowers, says she can't fight it another day...

What about the phoenix?

She sits with me in the darkness. She whispers, "We'll rise. Just you wait."

The legend of the phoenix speaks of a mythical bird with the power to live eternally via rising (resurrection) throughout the ages. Originally from Greek mythology, the phoenix now stands as a Christian symbol of eternal life, of the ability to live despite what might try to destroy.

I believe it is for this reason we don't hear as much about the phoenix as we should. We are quick to gravitate to the wolf that seems to have aggressive fighting power, the dragon that blows fire, and the lioness who roars and charges when threatened. We love the idea of aggression solving all our problems and think if we can just take enough charge, be threatening enough, or fight hard enough, everything will work in our favor. We forget that every story has its ending, and many stories wrought in aggression don't have happy endings. There is something to be said for sitting still, waiting out divine timing, and trusting God that our resurrection awaits, even if it means we sit out the battle because we know it is one that is not for us to fight.

While the Phoenix is a mythological image, resurrection is not lore from a begotten era. It is a reality, something we see as a type or shadow moving throughout the entirety of our lives. Resurrection is often discussed as the ultimate story of overcoming: Nothing, not even death, can overcome the power of eternal life. This is factual, but resurrection isn't something we await for the time our literal death. Throughout our lives we see the pattern of resurrection present as God revives things we thought were gone, dead, or replaces old things with new, living ones. In resurrection, God brings us to life again. Nothing is permanent as we embrace the idea that God is our change; He changes not because He is change. God is there, speaking to us constantly, switching and shifting things to bring us back to life in what seems dead or done. He is our great reviver, the source of the greatest revival; that which redeems the wayward soul that has had enough and can't fathom a better day to come.

Both trials and ordinary days drag on our experience and cause us to put away the dreams, visions, and ideas that fill us with promise and hope. Bills must be paid, family matters fill our minds, issues with health arise, jobs are lost or changed, friends come and go, and those closest to us are absent in the body, but present with the Lord. We are reduced to ashes; to a place where we think we will never recover. We forget who we are, we forget who we are called to be. God comes and revives, not with a growl, nor breathing fire, nor the roar of a lion, but the quiet voice that renews and resurrects the things we assume are dead. As our change, God resurrects, expands, continues, and shifts our vision, reminding us that nothing is dead when we have Him.

On days like today, I hear the phoenix speaking to me in the ashes I feel around me. She calls, she promises. She reminds me of the truth I too easily forget.

"Yeah girl, we got this. We'll rise. Just you wait."

But in His own seasons manifested His word
in the message, wherewith I was intrusted
according to the commandment of God our Savior.
(Titus 1:3, ASV)

Twenty-Eight

IT'S A NEW SEASON COMING TO BE

Daniel answered, Blessed be the Name of God forever and ever! For wisdom and might are His! He changes the times and the seasons; He removes kings and sets up kings. He gives wisdom to the wise and knowledge to those who have understanding! He reveals the deep and secret things; He knows what is in the darkness, and the light dwells with Him!
(Daniel 2:20-22)

I once heard a story about the way different plants survive after forest fires. It was fascinating to me to note the way that different species not only survive, but often go on to thrive in such extreme conditions. Pyrophytic plants (certain types of pine and eucalyptus) produce seeds or fruits completely sealed by resin, meaning they can only open to release their seeds after fire melts the resin. This means fire is actually required for these plants to reproduce. Some plants survive due to thermal insulation (such as sequoias) present within their own bark or leaves. They fight the burn by providing both protection and moisture. Science has also discovered that some trees are biologically programmed to resprout when burned or to flower in the aftermath, due to the chemical compounds found in fire ash.

I don't believe this is a story of triumph over destruction, as some people make it out to be. These stories are often used to tell people that they can overcome anything, even the "fires" of life. While I think there's nothing wrong with this message, it doesn't consider the fact that at some point in time, the "fire" of life will return. For as long as we are here, there will be the changing of seasons, as well as things that arise within seasons that fall out of line with the normal course of operation (using the seasonal metaphor: unexpected drought, poor harvest, natural disaster, and so on). The way by which these plants not only survive, but flourish during the most extreme conditions imaginable, proves that God's design provided for the fact that a certain level of flexibility is required to pass from one season to another.

We love the idea of triumphing over issues and never having to confront them – or new ones – ever again. The idea that pain with pleasure, suffering with contentment, and good with evil often work as tradeoffs this side of both heaven and the second coming isn't a fact we like to accept in the cyclical nature of life, but unfortunately, they are. There will never come a time before we make it to heaven or before Jesus comes back by which we will triumph over every problem we have. Just as we need good times, we also need the confrontations of the bad to make us flexible in life and spirit.

New seasons don't signify a lack of problems; they signify survival. We must be able to adapt through harsh conditions, the unexpected, the uncomfortable, and the difficult to make it through to something else. As uncomfortable as it may be, we can't confront the unknown in the new if we can't survive. God has given us the ability and mechanism, in the midst of trial, fire, and the unexpected, to pass from season to season as long as we are part of His greater plan. No matter what comes, it does not destroy, but transitions us through to whatever He has next.

As we sit and doubt (or in this situation, sit and pout through this devotion, as it's not what any of us expected), we may just be surprised at what flourishes – blooms – and begins when seasons shift. There's always something both different and familiar in new seasons; something that brings the echoes of seeds past and current growth, as well as something that transitions us into the position and place we are called to be right now, right in this moment.

New seasons teach us the importance of placement. We are here for a reason, even if we don't understand it. This forces us to stretch our sights to eternity; bigger than our trials, bigger than our difficulties, bigger than what might be happening as things burn and survive around us, yet again, and again, and again. The new season comes to be because the old cannot contain all it has stored up for this moment. It is the right time, and the right day for the new to begin.

FOR PERHAPS HE WAS THEREFORE PARTED FROM THEE FOR A SEASON, THAT THOU SHOULDEST HAVE HIM FOR EVER; NO LONGER AS A SERVANT, BUT MORE THAN A SERVANT, A BROTHER BELOVED...

(PHILEMON 1:15-16, ASV)

Afterword

EMBRACING WHAT'S NEW

Behold, I am doing a new thing! Now it springs forth;
do you not perceive and know it and will you not give heed to it?
I will even make a way in the wilderness and rivers
in the desert.
(Isaiah 43:19)

There was a time when the words, "It's your season!" bellowed from the pulpit with an air of excitement and awe. It was considered the "word" to get because we assumed it meant we would be met with the greatest time of our lives...one of endless manifestation and happiness. We also got the implied message that we would finally stop dealing with things that we disliked, and we would now successfully walk away from them, never to return.

I don't think it's beyond anyone's imagination to realize an awful lot of us never got these promised "seasons," no matter how many people told us they were spiritual word. We didn't get them because God never promised us an endless season that lacks the realities of growth and maturity from a spiritual perspective. What I have come to see since is that all seasons we are in are our seasons...we just don't like them all. Good and bad seasons alike have their purpose and while we don't like the seasons that grow and stretch us, they are just as important as the ones that seem to bless and encourage us as we aspire to new heights.

Maybe more than the idea of separate seasons for everything in life that seem opposite, my perspective today is far more non-binary than it was in years past. Every season has little pieces of various aspects of seasonal life contained within them. In every season, we plant something; we wait for something to grow; the thing that actually grows is usually us; we harvest some; and we reflect a whole lot as we enjoy both struggle and progress when things go wrong and right alike.

I've also discovered that seasons often change when we least expect. For the season I was in prior to this book, I was forced to embrace the darker parts of myself that I tried to avoid. I thought it was a season that was never going to end, feeling like the darkness permeated me in a way that was uncomfortable and awkward. Initially, I fought it, hoping that by doing so, it would vanish. It was a long-fought struggle to embrace what was and realize that by doing such, I was coming to accept parts of myself that I tried to pretend didn't exist. When I came to a place of this acceptance, the season shifted without a lot of fanfare, without a great sense of release or change, and without much to say in general. It passed, much like seasons do in the natural: days gradually got lighter, days got warmer, and change came as God made His presence known in unexpected ways without first announcing His arrival.

When the seasons changed, I didn't abandon the darker parts of myself; I embraced them and connected with them in a new way. They are part of me, after all. To embrace what is new, I had to embrace all of me, seeing the dark as necessary as the light and without a moral filter that narrated the dark as bad and the light as good. God is present in the dark as much as the light, we must just rest in the unknown as we await His presence manifest in the treasures of darkness.

With the conclusion of *Healing Times*, my Spiritual Darkness trilogy is closed. I have made peace with the darker parts of myself in personality and being. I needed all three phases to write, transform, and re-develop as a person who didn't want to reinvent themselves this additional time. These three books stand as my memories through them, speaking to you as you work to embrace the darker parts of yourself and move toward not a better day, but a different one.

As we pass from season to season, all we remember are moments; all we take are seeds for us to plant as new things begin. Let us embrace our new, scary as it is. Let us walk in our seasons, seeing day and night as essential to our purpose. Let's take our discouragement and hope alike and know that every season is for us...even if we stand among the ashes of dreams past and dig up the dirt again to plant, asking God to help us through our unbelief as He promises us all things are possible, once more.

References

[1]Holmes, Kenneth. "Just for Today." *Al-Anon Family Groups of South Carolina*. https://www.al-anon-sc.org/just-for-today.html. Accessed February 4, 2023.

[2]Niebuhr, Reinhold. Full Version Serenity Prayer, The. Serenity Prayer. https://www.prayerfoundation.org/dailyoffice/serenity_prayer_full_version.htm. Public Domain. Accessed February 15, 2023.

Other Books of Interest By the Author

- *A Heart God Can Use: The Journey to the Center of His Will* (Remnant Words, 2018)
- *Between the Porch and the Altar: A Journey Through the Book of Joel* (Righteous Pen Publications, 2016)
- *Call Me Bitter: Devotions for the Hurting* (Remnant Words, 2022)
- *Manifestations of the Spirit: The Work of the Holy Spirit in the Church and in Your Life* (Righteous Pen Publications, 2019)
- *Power for Today: Practical Spirituality for Everyday Living* (Volume 1) (Righteous Pen Publications, 2016)
- *Seeds for the Season: 91 Days of Breakthrough* (Righteous Pen Publications, 2018)
- *Waiting...Devotions for the Journey* (Remnant Words, 2020)

About the Author

These that have turned the world upside down
are come hither also.
(Acts 17:6, KJV)

Dr. Lee Ann B. Marino, Ph.D., D.Min., D.D. (she/her) is "everyone's favorite theologian" leading Gen X, Millennials, and Gen Z with expertise in leadership training, queer and feminist theology, general religion, and apostolic theology. She has served in ministry since 1998 and was ordained as a pastor in 2002 and an apostle in 2010. She founded what is now Sanctuary Apostolic Fellowship Empowerment (SAFE) Ministries in 2004. Under her ministry heading Dr. Marino is founder and Overseer of Sanctuary International Fellowship Tabernacle (SIFT) (the original home of National Coming Out Sunday) and The Sanctuary Network, and Chancellor of Apostolic Covenant Theological Seminary (ACTS).

Affectionately nicknamed "the Spitfire," Dr. Marino has spent over two decades as an "apostle, preacher, and teacher" (2 Timothy 1:11), exercising her personal mandate to become "all things to all people" (1 Corinthians 9:22). Her embrace of spiritual issues (both technical and intimate) has found its home among both seekers and believers, those who desire spiritual answers to today's issues.

Dr. Marino has preached throughout the United States, Puerto Rico, and Europe in hundreds of religious services and experiences throughout the years. A history maker in her own right, she has spent over two decades in advocacy, education, and work for and within minority spiritual communities (including African American, Hispanic, and LGBTQ+). She has also served as the first woman on all-male synods, councils, and panels, as well as the first preacher or speaker welcomed of a different race, sexual orientation, or identity among diverse communities. Today, Dr. Marino's work extends to over 150 countries as she hosts the popular *Kingdom Now* podcast, which is in the top 20 percentile of all podcasts worldwide. She is also the author of over 35 books and the popular Patheos column, *Leadership on Fire*. She was honored to be a Patheos Featured Writer in April 2026. To date, she has had five bestselling titles within their subject matter: *Understanding Demonology, Spiritual Warfare, Healing, and Deliverance: A Manual for the Christian Minister*; *Ministry School Boot Camp: Training for Helps Ministries, Appointments, and Beyond*; *Discovering Intimacy: A Journey Through the Song of Solomon*; *Fruit of the Vine: Study and Commentary on the Fruit of the Spirit*; and *Ministering to LGBTQ+ (and Those Who Love Them): A Primer for Queer Theology* (and its accompanying workbook).

As a public icon and social media influencer, Dr. Marino advocates healthy body image (curvy/full-figured), representation as a demisexual/aromantic, and albinism awareness as a model. Known to those she works with, she is a spiritual mom, teacher, leader, professor, confidant, and friend. She continues to transform, receiving new teaching, revelation, and insight in this thing we call "ministry." Through years of spiritual growth and maturity, Dr. Marino stands as herself, here to present what God has given to her for any who have an ear to hear.

For more information, visit her website at kingdompowernow.org.

www.ingramcontent.com/pod-product-compliance
Lightning Source LLC
LaVergne TN
LVHW010103110826
845155LV00028B/463